Pelargoniums

KEW GARDENING GUIDES

Pelargoniums

David Clark

Series editor John Simmons
M.Hort. (RHS), F.I. Hort., C.Biol., M.I. Biol.

The Royal Botanic Gardens, Kew
in association with
COLLINGRIDGE

Front cover photograph by David Clark ('Paton's Unique')
Back cover photograph by The Harry Smith Horticultural Photographic Collection

Published in 1988 by Collingridge Books
an imprint of The Hamlyn Publishing Group Limited,
Michelin House, 81 Fulham Road, London SW3 6RB
in association with The Royal Botanic Gardens, Kew.

ISBN 0 600 555 81 X

Filmset in England by Vision Typesetting, Manchester
in 11 on 12 pt Bembo

Printed in Spain

Contents

Preface

The Royal Botanic Gardens, Kew with their herbarium, library, laboratories and unrivalled collection of living plants, form one of the world's most important centres of botanical science. Their origins, however, can be traced back to a modest nine-acre site in the Pleasure Garden at Kew which Augusta, the Dowager Princess of Wales and mother of King George III, set aside for the cultivation of new and interesting plants.

On this site were grown many of the exotic species which reached England for the first time during this period of mercantile and colonial expansion. Trees such as our oldest specimens of *Sophora japonica* from China and *Robinia pseudoacacia* from America were planted for the Princess and still flourish at Kew, as do many accessions from Africa and Australia.

Many of Kew's earliest collectors were botanical explorers who made difficult and dangerous journeys to remote and unknown parts of the world in their search for economically important or beautiful plants. The work of Kew's botanists in gathering new species was complemented by that of Kew's gardeners, who were responsible for their care and propagation. The gardeners were also responsible for trans-shipping living plants from Kew to other parts of the world, and the Gardens rapidly became a clearing house through which 'useful' species grown in one continent were transferred to another.

At the present time, the living collections of the Royal Botanic Gardens contain approximately 50,000 types of flowering plants from every corner of the earth. Such a collection makes unending demands on the skills and dedication of those entrusted with its care. It also provides an unrivalled opportunity for gardening staff to familiarize themselves with the diverse requirements of plants from the many different climatic and geological regions of the world. The plants in the Royal Botanic Gardens are no museum collection, however. As in the eighteenth and nineteenth centuries, the Gardens continue to distribute living plant material on a worldwide basis, though they now use modern facilities such as the micropropagation unit at Kew and the Seed Bank at Wakehurst Place. The Gardens are also actively involved in the conservation of the world's plant resources and in supplying scientists at Kew and elsewhere with the plants and plant material required for their research. This may range from basic studies of the ways in which plants have evolved to the isolation of plant chemicals of potential use in agriculture and medicine. Whatever the purpose of the research, there is inevitably a need to grow plants and to grow them well, whether they be plants from the rain forests of the Amazon or from the deserts of Africa.

Your interest in gardening may be neither scientific nor economic, but I believe that the expert advice provided by specialist authors in this new series of *Kew Gardening Guides* will provide help of a quality that can be given only by gardeners with long experience of the art and science of cultivating a particular group of plants.

E. Arthur Bell
Director, Royal Botanic Gardens, Kew

Opposite:
Pelargonium tricolor
plate number 240
from *Botanical Magazine* (see page 93)

Foreword

Gardening is in part instinctive, in part experience. Look in any village or town and you will see many gardens, balconies or even windowsills full of healthy plants brightening up the streets. However, there are always likely to be other plots that are sterile and devoid of plants, or overgrown and unloved. Admittedly gardening is laborious, but the hours spent sweating behind a mower on a hot summer's day will be amply rewarded when the smooth green lawn is admired; the painful nettle stings incurred while clearing ground will soon be forgotten when the buds of newly planted shrubs burst forth in spring.

These few examples of the joy and pain of gardening are all part of its attraction to its devotees. The successful gardeners and plant lovers of this world come to understand plants instinctively, learning their likes and dislikes, their lifespan and ultimate size, recognizing and correcting ailments before they become serious. They work with the seasons of the year, not against them; they think ahead, driven by caring, being aware of when conditions are right for planting, mowing or harvesting and, perhaps most important of all, they know when to leave well alone.

This understanding of the natural order cannot be learned overnight. It is a continuous two-way process that lasts a lifetime. In creating a garden, past masters such as Humphry Repton in the eighteenth century or Gertrude Jekyll in the nineteenth perceived and enhanced the natural advantages of a site, and Jekyll in particular was an acute observer of the countryside and its seasons. Seeing a plant in its natural situation gives knowledge of its needs in cultivation. And then, once design and planting have formed a garden, the process reverses as the garden becomes the inspiration for learning about the natural world.

With the widespread loss of the world's natural habitats now causing the daily extinction of species, botanic gardens and other specialist gardens are becoming as arks, holding irreplaceable collections. Thus gardens are increasingly cooperating to form networks which can retain as great a diversity of plants as possible. More than ever gardens can offer a refuge for our beleaguered flora and fauna and, whether a garden be great or small, formal or natural, this need should underpin its enduring qualities of peace and harmony – the challenge of the creative unison of formal and natural areas.

The authors of these volumes have all become acknowledged specialists in particular aspects of gardening and their texts draw on their experience and impart the vitality that sustains their own enthusiasm and dedication. It is hoped, therefore, that these *Kew Gardening Guides* will be the means of sharing their hard-earned knowledge and understanding with a wider audience.

Like a many faceted gemstone, horticulture has many sides, each with its own devotees, but plants are the common link, and they define this series of horticultural books and the work of Kew itself.

John Simmons
Editor

Introduction

Pelargoniums are versatile and popular plants. In spite of the fact that in some circles they are regarded as too commonplace and ordinary to be taken seriously, they can be found throughout the world. Anyone who has taken a holiday in mainland Europe will have noticed that pelargoniums dominate displays in virtually every balcony and window box.

In Victorian England these plants were highly prized, but as a result of the ravages and changes of opinion following the the First World War, they started to decline in popularity. Many growers like a challenge, and pelargoniums suffer from being commonplace and too easy to grow – the very virtues that make them so popular to many other gardeners.

Few other groups of plants can claim to be so well known and so adaptable, yet 'Freak of Nature', introduced in 1880, with white stems and green-centred white leaves, is still shrouded in mystery. Modern science still has no explanation for the existence of a plant that reverses the normal mode of coloration.

A great deal of work has been carried out by research stations, seedsmen, large commercial nurseries, etc. to determine the ideal conditions for growing pelargoniums. Where possible, figures have been quoted to support the recommended methods described in this book. Loose and vague terms that mean different things to different people have been avoided. When careful experimentation has revealed that the optimum temperature for germinating pelargonium seed is between 21 and 24°C (70–75°F), why use the terms warm or fairly warm?

Traditionally pelargoniums have been propagated from cuttings, but work originating in the USA in the 1950s gave birth to the modern seed-raised strains that are now used by virtually all municipal authorities for their large-scale bedding plant displays. Modern plant hybridists have also worked wonders in creating many new plants with eyecatching beauty, in shades of colour that would have astounded Victorian collectors. Yellow flowers are not unknown among pelargoniums, but nobody has yet produced a really first-rate cultivar in a shade of buttercup yellow.

To look to the future, it is almost certain that seed-raised strains of double flowered zonal and ivy leaf pelargoniums will continue to make inroads into those produced by traditional methods of propagation, and no doubt new and appealing colours will be produced, including the perfect yellow-flowered cultivar. One thing is certain: whatever the future holds, there will be enthusiasts growing pelargoniums throughout the world; and it would be surprising if they were not among the first ornamental plants to travel the solar system if man eventually colonizes other planets.

1
History, Botany and Nomenclature

After the foundation of the Dutch East India Company in 1602 the Cape of Good Hope became an important point on the route between India and The Netherlands. In 1652 a colony was established 50 km (30 miles) to the north that became the modern city of Cape Town. Many authorities attribute the first introduction of pelargoniums into Europe to the Dutch governor of the Cape Colony, who sent a *Pelargonium* species to Holland in 1700. However, the Earl of Portland had *P. capitatum* in cultivation in 1690, the year in which it was first described. (In Webb (1984.4): 'A revision of Gerard's *Herebal* was brought out in 1633 by Thomas Johnson, who made the first reference to a South African species of the genus *Pelargonium*. Johnson wrote that he had seen the plant in bloom in the previous summer, 1632, in the garden of John Tradescant of Lambeth and refers to the species as a rare and beautiful plant called *Geranium Indicum Noctu Odoratum*. His description is so accurate that there is no doubt that the plant is what is called today *P. triste*.') The Cape Colony was finally captured by the British in 1806 after a brief earlier occupation.

At this time a great many species were imported into Britain. In 1732 J.J. Dillenius, the first Professor of Botany at Oxford University, published a work entitled *Hortus Elthamensis*, which described a number of African pelargoniums growing in the garden of Dr James Sherard at Eltham near London.

There have been peaks of interest in growing pelargoniums, notably in the early 19th century, the late Victorian period and at the present time. Interest in pelargoniums and many other ornamental plants declined during and after both world wars.

The hybridization of pelargoniums has continued throughout this period, and steady and sometimes spectacular progress has been made. Zonal pelargonium seed has been available commercially from at least one British seed company since 1909, and in the 1950s Professor Graig of Pennsylvania State University, USA, started a breeding programme that has led to the success of the modern seed-raised strains.

There is a great deal of debate among growers about whether these plants should be called geraniums or pelargoniums. However, it is currently agreed that all the plants described in this book belong to the genus *Pelargonium*. Difficulty has arisen because before this genus had been defined many of the plants were called *Geranium*, a name that is now used for a related but distinctly different group of plants. Unfortunately the old name is still being used for some pelargoniums, especially the typically scarlet-flowered bedding or pot plant.

It is confusing to use geranium as the common term for the entire family when within that family the same name is used scientifically for a particular genus. The distinction in spelling (geranium in common usage, *Geranium* in scientific terms) cannot be made with the spoken word. Despite these obvious disadvantages there are a number of growers who wish to retain the use of the word geranium to describe particular pelargoniums. The public are used to calling regal

Opposite:
Pelargonium tomentosum plate number 518 from *Botanical Magazine* (see page 93)

pelargoniums by their correct name, so the recent movement towards calling them regal geraniums is hardly helpful. While the name geranium is being used indiscriminately there will always be confusion, and where there is confusion there will continue to be controversy. Unfortunately, while the name geranium slips easily off the tongue, pelargonium is undoubtedly an ugly word and more difficult to pronounce. Could this be the real cause of the problem?

The botanical genus *Geranium* is widespread throughout the temperate regions of the world, whereas *Pelargonium* species are restricted almost entirely to certain warm temperate or subtropical areas. Most of the species are found growing in South Africa, but some occur in New Zealand, Australia, and a few small, isolated islands. These habitats are all very arid and dry, at least for part of the year; many species are succulent and live in desert regions.

The true *Geranium* species have ten fertile stamens and the flowers are regular in shape, whereas those of the *Pelargonium* have irregular flowers with up to seven of the ten stamens being fertile, and the structure has the added feature of a nectar spur. Other botanical features are shown in the illustration.

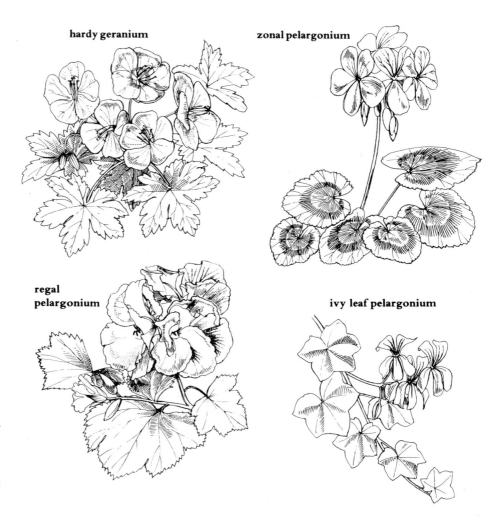

hardy geranium

zonal pelargonium

regal pelargonium

ivy leaf pelargonium

The appearance of a hardy geranium compared with three typical examples from the genus *Pelargonium*

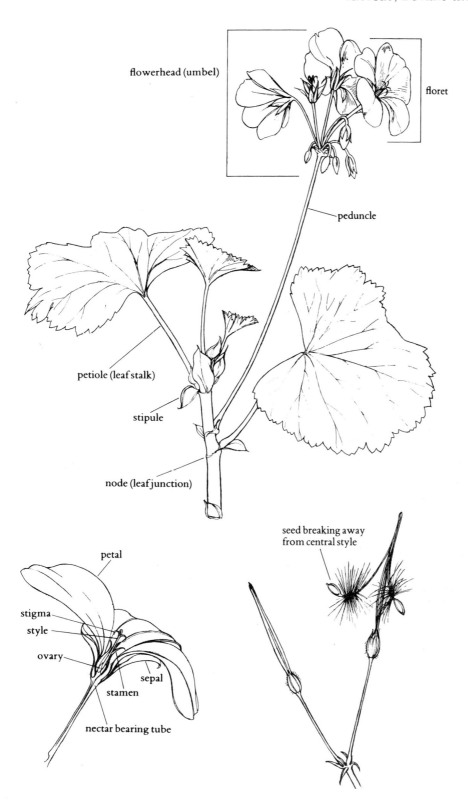

flowerhead (umbel)

floret

Parts of a zonal pelargonium. Enthusiasts often refer to the individual florets as 'pips'

peduncle

petiole (leaf stalk)

stipule

node (leaf junction)

seed breaking away from central style

petal

stigma

style

ovary

sepal

stamen

nectar bearing tube

Far left: A cross-section through a typical pelargonium flower

Left: The distinctive fruit of a pelargonium

PELARGONIUM SPECIES

The genus *Pelargonium* is a large and diverse group of plants; the botanical classification is very confused, and there are a lot more names than there are distinct species. Over the years botanists have proposed various systematic changes to the family, and the problems are compounded by the great variation among many species and the common occurrence of natural hybrids. Many species do not appeal to the general public, so they may be grown and sold only by a few specialist nurserymen. However, some of the more popular kinds have scented leaves, and others are available with attractive variegated leaves. Pelargoniums live in arid areas where vegetation is sparse, and the strongly scented foliage, which is distasteful to animals, gives considerable protection. Many species are adapted to withstand long periods of drought: they are succulents, and have stems that are thickened or roots that have become swollen to assist with water storage.

SCENTED LEAF PELARGONIUMS

This group contains species that have scented foliage, and the many hybrids that have been produced by crossing these and other taxa with each other. *P. crispum* and *P. graveolens* have produced many interesting plants, whereas *P. tomentosum* and *P. odoratissimum* have contributed only to a lesser extent. The flowers of this group are often considered of secondary importance, but many of them are very attractive.

Opposite: Scented leaf pelargoniums in the herb garden

Right: *Pelargonium × kewense* (see pages 20 and 93)

HYBRIDS

Hybrids are produced by crossing two taxa together, and they often occur naturally in the wild or in collections in cultivation. In the latter instance the most famous example is that of *P. × kewense*, which was found at the Royal Botanic Gardens, Kew and described in 1934.

REGAL PELARGONIUMS

The term regal pelargonium (*Pelargonium × domesticum*) covers a large group of plants that were once variously called 'Show', 'Grandiflora', 'Large Flowered', 'Decorative' and 'Fancy' pelargoniums. In the United States they have also been called 'Martha' or 'Lady Washington' pelargoniums. Although the public usually recognizes these plants correctly as pelargoniums, some authorities refer to them as regal geraniums.

This group of plants has slightly hairy leaves that are either odourless or have a faint, pleasant smell. The leaves do not have a zone and the edges are serrated. Each floret is large, and usually carries between five and nine petals; each flowerhead is composed of five or more florets. The flowers open flat or are slightly bell shaped, but often they cannot open fully because of lack of space in the flowerhead. Although many cultivars have more than five petals to each floret they are arranged in the same plane as the other petals, so the overall appearance of the flower is not greatly altered and they are not regarded as double. However, the petals are often ruffled, which gives an impression of their being double. At least one fully double form has been described, but because of its poor growth habit it never became popular.

The ancestry of these plants is complex and speculative, as most of the original crosses were not recorded or the details have been lost. The most important species involved are thought to be *P. cucullatum* (*P. angulosum*), *P. grandiflorum*, *P. capitatum* and *P. fulgidum*. Most of the older regal pelargoniums flower only once each spring, but the more modern kinds are repeat flowering and will continue to produce a succession of blooms into winter.

ANGEL PELARGONIUMS

These are classified as miniature regal pelargoniums, and are included with the previous section under the exhibition rules of many of the specialist societies. The flowers are on average about 2.5 cm (1 in) in diameter, and bear a strong resemblance to regal pelargoniums. The stems are thin and the leaves small; the plants can be contained in a small pot for a while, but they will eventually grow quite large.

The name of this group is thought to have derived from 'Angeline', a dwarf pelargonium no longer in cultivation. Many of the plants included in this group were raised by Arthur Langley Smith. The strain was obtained by crossing *P. crispum* with 'The Shah', an early regal pelargonium. The name 'Miniature Regal Pelargonium' sits uneasily on this group of plants; their appearance and ancestry sets them apart and they are not true miniature forms of regal pelargoniums.

Unique pelargoniums

These are large growing, shrubby plants that develop woody stems. The leaves are often deeply lobed, and although they sometimes have a pleasant smell they can often be quite unpleasant. The medium-sized flowers are only sparsely produced, and are in shades of red, white, pink and mauve.

The plural 'Uniques' is unfortunately used to describe this group. Their ancestry is uncertain, but it is thought that *P. fulgidum* played an important part.

Zonal pelargoniums

This large and diverse group of cultivars is officially known as *Pelargonium × hortorum*. It is customary to classify them in a number of ways, partly to help nurserymen group together plants with similar characteristics, and partly for purposes of competitive exhibition. These groups have traditionally been made on the basis of the form of the flowers, e.g. single, double, rosebud or cactus; on the colour of the leaves – green, gold, bicoloured or tricoloured; or on whether the height of the plant is normal, dwarf or miniature. A few decades ago it was justifiable to separate cultivars that were grown primarily for their flowers from those that were grown for their decorative foliage, as in general the latter group had rather insignificant blooms. However, modern hybridists have improved the size, quality and colour range in some of the decorative foliage groups, so they too are now worth growing for the flowers alone. Many cultivars will now fit into several different categories. For example, 'Golden Ears' is a member of the stellar group, it also has bronze foliage, and it is dwarf.

Although these plants are divided into normal, dwarf and miniature sizes there is infinite gradation within each group. A well-grown specimen of the miniature 'Royal Norfolk' can easily grow into the dwarf category, and, conversely, one of the smaller dwarf cultivars might remain miniature unless given reasonably good growing conditions. In the light of modern developments it can be seen that the old methods of classifying these plants are under considerable strain, and no attempt has been made to adopt this approach in the lists of cultivars in this book (see page 91ff). Zonal pelargoniums are listed later in this section by their individual characteristics, but many modern cultivars will fit into more than one category.

The true ancestry of zonal pelargoniums, in common with the other groups, has not been recorded, but *P. inquinans*, *P. zonale*, *P. hybridum* and *P. frutetorum* have all played their part. Although red-flowered cultivars are very common this colour is rare among the species, so it is safe to presume that the red-flowered *P. inquinans* and *P. zonale* have played an important part in their formation.

Single flowered group
These are cultivars that have florets composed of five petals. 'Highfield's Pride' and most of the F_1 hybrid seed-raised strains are typical examples.

Semi-double and double flowered group
These are cultivars that have florets composed of more than five petals; semi-double flowers may have five petals plus some extra, partially formed petals. The

Pelargonium peltatum (see page 93)

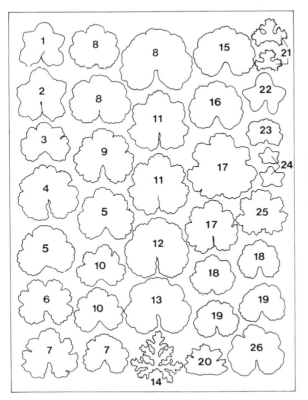

Key to foliage display

1 'White Mesh'
2 'Magaluf'
3 'Friary Wood'
4 'Susie Q'
5 'Contrast'
6 'Maréchal MacMahon'
7 'A Happy Thought'
8 'Mrs H. Cox'
9 'Golden Crest'
10 'Turkish Delight'
11 'Skies of Italy'
12 'Mrs Quilter'
13 'Falklands Hero'
14 'Lady Plymouth'
15 'Chelsea Gem'
16 'Patchwork Quilt'
17 'Mrs Pollock'
18 'Miss Burdett-Coutts'
19 'Lass O'Gowrie'
20 'Golden Ears'
21 *P. crispum*
   'Variegatum'
22 'Lilac Gem'
23 'Frank Headley'
24 'Flakey'
25 'Distinction'
26 'Deacon Peacock'

dividing line between these two groups is difficult to define exactly, as cultivation conditions can to some extent alter the doubleness of a flower, so that semi-double flowers can become fully double and vice versa. 'Irene' is a typical semi-double, and 'Regina' is a superb double-flowered cultivar.

Rosebud group
These are very fully double flowers, so tightly packed with petals that the centre of the flower looks like a miniature rosebud. 'Apple Blossom Rosebud' is a typical member of this group.

Cactus flowered group
The flowers have curious petals that are rolled into a quill shape. The flowers can be single or double. 'Spitfire' is a member of this group and also has bicoloured leaves.

Green leaf group
This is the normal state but the leaves may have a well-defined dark zone, or it may be absent. The leaves can be pale green or blackish green.

Gold leaf group
The leaves are typically a clear golden yellow colour. Sometimes the leaf is unzoned, but there is often a noticeable bronze zone. Quite where the plant stops being a member of the gold leaf group and becomes member of the bicoloured leaf group (bronze/gold) is a matter for conjecture. The leaf colour often varies considerably as it is affected by the intensity of light and by nutrition. In winter, low light levels cause the leaves to change to a greenish hue, as does overfeeding or feeding with a fertilizer that has a high nitrogen content. A typical and very beautiful member of this group is 'Hunter's Moon'.

Bicoloured leaf group
These plants may have green and cream, green and white, bronze and green, or bronze and gold leaves. There are many cultivars that will fit this classification. The remarks about changes in leaf colour made in the preceding group also apply here.

Tricoloured leaf group
These plants have multicoloured leaves that can be described in shades of three main colours. One is a shade of green; another either white, cream or yellow; the third a shade of bright red or brownish-red or a mixture of the two. The most famous member of this group is 'Mrs H. Cox'.

Miniature zonal pelargoniums
These are plants that mature naturally at a small size. For exhibition purposes the height of the foliage above the top of the pot should not exceed 13 cm (5 in). Single and double flowered forms are available, as are those with gold, bicoloured and tricoloured foliage.

Dwarf zonal pelargoniums

These plants should not exceed 20 cm (8 in) from the top of the pot to the top of the foliage. Virtually all the coloured leaf forms and the other variations are found in this group.

Seed-raised zonal pelargoniums

These plants are relatively new, and are often used by parks departments and other municipal authorities for massed bedding displays. The plants grown are usually F_1 hybrids and have single flowers, but a few non F_1 strains have been marketed that produce a proportion of double blooms. (For fuller details of these plants see F_1 hybrid seed production in the chapter on cultivation on page 73.)

IVY LEAF PELARGONIUMS

The leaves of ivy leaf pelargoniums (*P. peltatum*) bear a resemblance to those of ivy (*Hedera helix*), and some cultivars, such as 'Lilac Gem', also smell strongly of ivy. The leaves are often shiny, and some cultivars have a dark zone in the centre. The stems are usually long and trailing though some, such as 'Sybil Holmes' and 'Sugar Baby', are bushy and compact. In the wild *P. peltatum* is a very variable species, and some authorities believe that this group has been derived entirely from the variations within this one plant. This is unlikely, however, and other species have probably contributed to its development.

Cultivars with single or double flowers and with variegated leaves are commonly available, as are some dwarf-growing types.

HYBRID IVY LEAF PELARGONIUMS

These are produced by crossing an ivy leaf pelargonium with a zonal pelargonium. Often the offspring (*P. peltatum* × *P.* × *hortorum*) has most of the character of the ivy leaf parent, but the growth is usually stiffer and more upright. However, some hybrids, notably the Deacon series, which has been produced by crossing a miniature zonal pelargonium with an ivy leaf cultivar, have entirely the character of a normal dwarf zonal pelargonium. For this reason the Deacons are grouped with zonal pelargoniums, though strictly they should be included in this section. This group can have double or single flowers and variegated leaf forms, and are available from specialist suppliers.

2
Uses of Pelargoniums

The species of the genus *Pelargonium* are diverse in character, and the hybrids that have been developed from them are even more remarkable in the different characteristics they possess. The property that all the species have in common, with perhaps one exception, is that they are all frost tender. This feature has been inherited by all the hybrids, and where winter temperatures fall below freezing, permanent planting out of doors is not possible. However, the majority of cultivars can withstand an occasional slight frost without serious damage.

PELARGONIUMS AS BEDDING PLANTS

A large proportion of zonal and ivy leaf pelargoniums is sold as bedding plants. Many tens of millions are bought worldwide. They are popular because they have very bright, attractive colours, a long flowering period and are very tolerant of neglect.

Some old gardening books will say that pelargoniums (they invariably refer to them as geraniums) only flower well in poor soil, but such statements cannot be substantiated. Any average garden soil will suit them admirably provided that it is well drained and not boggy. Very poor soils will be improved by the addition of garden compost, farmyard manure or any similar material that will increase its humus content. Very rich soils, such as old onion or asparagus beds, are not suitable as the plants grow large and leafy at the expense of the flowers. The acidity (pH) of the soil is not critical, but an alkaline soil is more easily tolerated than a very acid one. In common with most bedding plants, pelargoniums will benefit from the planting site being given the usual preliminary cultivation. The soil should be dug over and any additional compost or manure added at this stage, and if the soil is very poor a balanced fertilizer (see page 44) can be added at planting time. An exception can be made for the cultivars grown for their coloured leaves; these are always at their brightest when the plants are slightly starved, so extra fertilizer should not be added unless the soil is known to be very low in nutrients. In these circumstances a fertilizer that is high in potassium and low in nitrogen will give the best results.

The types of zonal pelargonium used in the past as bedding plants traditionally had green leaves and single red flowers. For this purpose the single or semi-double flowered cultivars are nearly always superior to the double flowered forms. Heads of double flowers contain many crevices that trap water, causing them to rot, but single or semi-double flowers shed water more easily. Damaged and dying heads of double flowered cultivars must be removed from the plants by hand or they will spoil the appearance of the display, but single flowered types drop their petals when they get old and are to a large extent self-cleaning.

Two cultivars that have been traditionally used for bedding are 'Paul Crampel' (single, red flowers) and 'Gustav Emich' (semi-double, red flowers). The latter was particularly famous because for many years it was used to make up

Opposite:
Pelargoniums are
the perfect plants
for growing in
containers and
hanging baskets

the display outside Buckingham Palace in London. These old cultivars were raised each year from cuttings and have now largely been replaced by the modern seed-raised strains. These new hybrids have not necessarily replaced the older ones because they are better, in fact many enthusiasts say emphatically they are not, but because they are cheaper to produce.

All pelargoniums are sun lovers, and they will grow best in open situations away from overhanging trees. The proximity of a wall facing south east or west is not a disadvantage as these positions are usually dry and warm.

The optimum planting distance will obviously vary depending on the habit and vigour of the cultivar chosen, but about 45 cm (18 in) is enough for the average bedding cultivar. It is always a mistake to plant mixed colours together or to interplant different cultivars in a haphazard manner. They will have uneven rates of growth and ultimately different heights, and the results will almost certainly be displeasing to the eye.

The zonal pelargonium not only makes an excellent flowering plant but also can excel as a decorative foliage plant. Massed beds of a tricoloured cultivar such as 'Mrs H. Cox' are outstandingly beautiful, and can more than rival traditional displays of flowers. Unfortunately such delights are very rarely seen today; the tricoloured leaf group are all slow growing, and cuttings need to be rooted early in the previous year so that they can be planted out as large, well-established specimens in the following spring. This is naturally a very costly procedure, and for this reason alone such displays are not often contemplated.

An alternative to the slow-growing tricolour group is the more vigorous silver bicoloured leaf group. Cultivars such as 'Caroline Schmidt' or 'Chelsea Gem' will grow strongly when bedded out, and have the added bonus of attractive foliage and flowers. Although these plants produce heads composed of double florets, they are smaller than those with the standard green leaves, and are less easily damaged by rain. Another alternative is to use coloured leaf cultivars as dot plants by interspersing them at regular intervals among the green-leaved ones to break up the uniformity of the display and to create more interest. A further development of this idea is to interplant standards of contrasting flower and leaf colour so that a variation in height is also introduced. Standards (see page 58) can make an excellent focal point or centrepiece of a display. A single standard in the centre of a circular bed of plants of contrasting colour is often more pleasing than an otherwise flat display. Ivy leaf pelargoniums can be trained as weeping standards, but because they can be very time-consuming to grow they are hardly ever seen except in the gardens of pelargonium enthusiasts. Standard pelargoniums also add grace to a patio display; they can be grown in large pots placed either side of a doorway, and will give a constant display of flower throughout the spring and summer with very little attention. A standard can also be planted in a large tub with plants offering contrasting flower or leaf colours planted around the base.

Miniature and dwarf zonal pelargoniums can also be used for bedding, but because of their diminutive size they are usually restricted to edging or to brighten temporary bare spots on a rock garden. Certain types of garden or patio walls are built with hollow tops that can be filled with soil; these areas are ideal for planting up with miniature or dwarf cultivars because the flowers are brought nearer to the observer's eye.

Although they are not often used as such, ivy leaf (trailing) pelargoniums make superb bedding plants. Their stems hug the ground and suppress the growth of many weeds. Because fewer plants are needed to fill a bed they are also more economical to use than the traditional zonal pelargonium. Some of the most suitable kinds for this purpose are the double flowered cultivars such as 'Galilee', 'La France', 'Tavira', 'Beauty of Eastbourne' or the more weather resistant single flowered cultivars such as members of the Balcon, Decora or Cascade groups.

Regal pelargoniums are not commonly used for bedding or for any other outdoor purpose. Their large flowers are badly damaged by heavy rain and strong winds, but in a good climate or a well-sheltered position they can make a spectacular display. To ensure that a good display of flowers is produced throughout the summer months the modern repeat flowering cultivars such as 'Pink Bonanza' are best for the purpose. In areas of unpredictable weather, such as the British Isles, regal pelargoniums can be disappointing when planted out of doors.

PELARGONIUMS IN THE HERB GARDEN

The more vigorous kinds of scented leaf pelargonium, such as *P. graveolens*, 'Lady Plymouth', 'Joy Lucille', 'Attar of Roses', etc., all grow fairly large when bedded out during the summer. Although they would not be listed among the top fifty most popular plants for the herb garden they should be considered worthy of inclusion. The leaves can be used to flavour a very wide range of foods including cakes and sponges, meat and fish dishes. The leaves can be used instead of, or to complement, the more traditional flavourings or to provide a source of natural material to avoid the use of synthetic substitutes. *P. graveolens*, *P. crispum* and 'Lady Plymouth' can be used to provide a subtle flavour of lemon, and 'Mabel Grey' provides a much stronger flavour. 'Attar of Roses' also imparts a flavour of lemon, but it has a subtle flavour of rose as well. *P. crispum* 'Variegatum' makes an outstandingly attractive, bushy plant and can easily be trained as a standard. These plants can therefore be used as a very attractive, scented plant in the house, greenhouse or conservatory, and also double as a herb for the kitchen. *P. fragrans* 'Variegata', also called 'Snowy Nutmeg', imparts a nutmeg flavour; *P. odoratissimum* has an apple flavour and blends well with recipes that use cider, adding an appealing extra freshness to the taste. *P. tomentosum* and 'Joy Lucille' can both be used to provide alternatives to synthetic peppermint flavourings. It is important to wash all leaves well before use and to make sure that the plants have not recently been treated with an insecticide. It is advisable to not use newly purchased plants for this purpose for at least one month in case the plant had been sprayed with a toxic chemical before being sold. Remember that these plants are usually marketed as decorative plants and are not necessarily considered as a food crop by the grower.

The leaves can be picked, placed loosely in paper bags and hung up to dry in a warm, airy place and used during the winter months instead of fresh material, or the plants can be grown in the herb garden in pots so that they can be moved into a frost-free greenhouse or conservatory for the winter. Freshly gathered leaves will, of course, always give the best results.

Zonal pelargoniums have long been used to brighten bedding displays in parks and gardens

Another very important use for scented leaf pelargoniums is in gardens for the blind. Although they are not all listed in this book some of the species and hybrids have variously been described as smelling of almonds, absinth, apple, balsam, cedar, chocolate, citron, nut, nutmeg, pepper, peppermint, pine and rose. With this wide range of odours and the varied shapes and textures of the leaves, pelargoniums should be considered an important part of the blind person's garden.

PELARGONIUMS IN CONTAINERS

Zonal and ivy leaf pelargoniums are excellent subjects for planting in tubs, urns, hanging baskets or other similar containers. They can be planted on their own or mixed with other plants such as lobelia, petunias, marigolds, etc. However, it is worth remembering that pelargoniums are much more tolerant of neglect than most other plants. In hot weather containers need regular watering, and if this cannot be attended to meticulously it would be better to omit the less tolerant

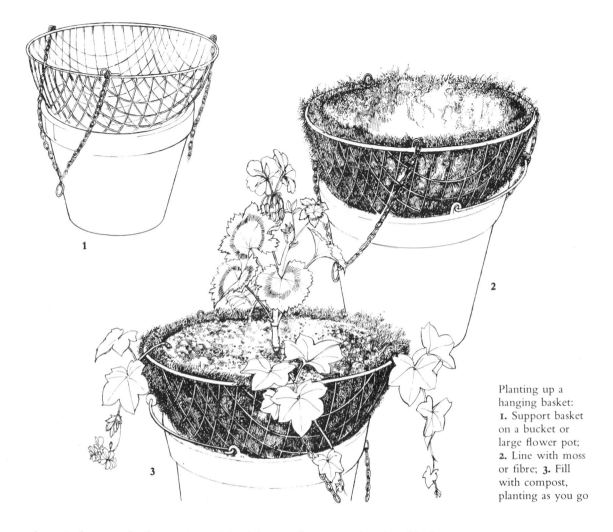

Planting up a hanging basket:
1. Support basket on a bucket or large flower pot; **2.** Line with moss or fibre; **3.** Fill with compost, planting as you go

plants in favour of pelargoniums. Upright zonal types can be placed in the centre of the container and the ivy leaf types allowed to trail over the sides. Variegated leaf forms can be used to add interest and contrast, so the omission of other bedding plants is not necessarily a loss.

The type of material that the containers are made from is not important. They can be constructed of any durable material such as wood, plastic, concrete or metal, but must all have plenty of holes in the base to facilitate drainage; pelargoniums will not tolerate waterlogged soil – nor will many other bedding plants. Because plants in containers have a restricted root run a good quality potting compost should be used. To save cost, some fertile and well-drained garden soils can be used, but worms and diseases are often introduced in this way and cause considerable damage in the confined space of a container. Not even a good quality potting compost will have sufficient nutrients to supply the needs of the plant for a whole season, so it will be necessary to feed them to encourage continuing growth and flower. Because soil-based (John Innes) potting composts generally have a greater reserve of plant nutrients than soilless composts they are usually preferred for this purpose. Some types of hanging pots or baskets need no special treatment, but those constructed of wire or plastic mesh need to be lined before they can be planted up. The lining can be moss, plastic sheeting or one of the proprietary products sold specially for the purpose. Despite being the most troublesome and time-consuming method, many growers still prefer the traditional moss-lined hanging basket. Plastic baskets and liners are made only in the smaller sizes, so if a large basket is required there may be no alternative but to use a moss-lined wire basket.

PELARGONIUMS IN THE HOUSE AND GREENHOUSE

Because of their great tolerance, pelargoniums make very long-lived houseplants. Although they will survive for long periods they are often leggy and sad looking, and their appearance may not be very attractive. There are a number of reasons why plants grow leggy in the home, the two principal ones being lack of light and the choice of an unsuitable cultivar. Pelargoniums are mostly sun lovers, and they must be grown in the brightest position possible. Close to the glass on a south-facing windowsill is an ideal position, and east- or west-facing situations are very much a second best choice. Some of the older cultivars will grow leggy even in a greenhouse, and these should not be selected for growing in the home where the intensity of illumination will be less. Many of the older zonal pelargoniums, such as 'Pride of the West', 'Kingswood' or 'Staplegrove Fancy', have not been bettered for their colouring and size of bloom, but they have tall, unbranching growth and have been replaced by more bushy, modern cultivars. The miniature and dwarf cultivars generally make excellent houseplants, their relatively small size being an asset in the average home.

The scented leaf pelargoniums, although they grow large, can also make good houseplants. They will need frequent trimming to control their size and shape, and as old plants tend to become woody, new ones will be required each year to replace them. Scented leaf pelargoniums propagate very easily so this should not cause undue difficulty (see page 67). In the home these plants act as a natural deodorizer and room freshener. Commercial deodorizing sprays work by releasing pleasant-smelling substances that seek out and tightly surround the molecules that are causing the unpleasant smell. This effectively replaces one smell by another. The natural oils contained in the pelargonium have this property, and the leaves need only to be brushed lightly with the hand to release the active substance into the air. *P. graveolens* is a good plant for this purpose, but to keep it bushy and attractive it should be grown close to the sunniest window of the room. In a similar way the dried leaves of these plants, together with dried rose petals, etc., can be used to make pot-pourri.

Young regal pelargoniums will also make good houseplants, but with age most of them will grow too large. 'Vicky Town' and 'Inca', however, are both naturally dwarf and are particularly suited to growing on a windowsill. Most regal pelargoniums are best grown in a greenhouse or conservatory where they can have enough space to attain full size. Some other cultivars, such as the dwarf zonal pelargonium 'Frank Headley', will produce a much greater quantity of flowers when grown under protection.

OTHER USES

Although they are not grown commercially, the blooms of zonal and ivy leaf pelargoniums are excellent cut flower subjects and last well in vases. The flowers should be picked by snapping them off or carefully cutting them from the main stem. The Victorians were fond of making complex flower arrangements using blooms of pelargoniums, fuchsias and other fashionable plants of the time.

The flowers are also particularly easy to preserve by drying them in silver sand mixed with either borax or silica gel. Young flowers or partially open flower buds are best for the purpose. Flowers and leaves can also be preserved by the familiar technique of pressing them in a special flower press. Leaves and flowers preserved by this technique can be used for making greeting cards, pictures, etc. Some people have great difficulty in growing ferns in the home, and the dried leaves of *P. filifolium* make an excellent easy-to-grow substitute for use in making dried flower pictures.

Apart from their use as decorative flowering and foliage plants, the only other major use of pelargoniums is for the production of 'geranium oil'. Although an oil can be extracted from one of the true *Geranium* species it is not carried out on a commercial scale, and the oil is produced entirely from pelargoniums. Oil of geranium, as it is known in the trade, is one of the most important ingredients in perfumery. The pure oil is almost a complete perfume in its own right, and it blends well with other ingredients to make floral and oriental scents. The odour lingers well and being chemically stable, particularly in mildly alkaline situations, it is frequently used for scenting soaps.

Pelargonium species were sent from their natural habitats by early collectors, particularly to the Royal Botanic Gardens at Kew. These species were extensively hybridized, and their descendants were distributed to various parts of Europe where they were sent to the colonies to found the new industry. The plants used for extraction of the essential oil are usually *P. graveolens* or a hybrid derived from this species. The odour of the crop is that of lemon grass oil, but as it comes into flower it changes to a strong rose-like smell, and at this stage the crop is harvested. The leaves are packed with some water into large stills and the mixture is boiled. The oil of geranium is distilled over with the steam and on cooling the oil is allowed to separate.

The industry started in the Grasse region of southern France in the early 19th century, and although very little is grown there today, oil from this source is still regarded as being of the highest quality. In 1847 plants were sent to Algeria to start an industry there, and in about 1880 plants from Grasse were sent to the island of Réunion in the Indian Ocean. Even today this is one of the island's most important exports. This crop has also been grown commercially in Corsica, Spain, Uganda, Kenya, Morocco and the USSR. Interestingly, although the same basic plant material was used by all producers, over a period of years, partly by natural selection and partly by human help, the oil from each area develops its own special character and is slightly different from that produced in other regions. A comparison can be made with wine production, where the soil and climate make subtle changes to the quality of the end product even though the type of grape grown in each area may be identical.

3
Cultivation

A large majority of pelargonium species are indigenous to South Africa, and their typical habitats are dry areas of desert or semi-desert. All plants that grow in these regions are adapted to withstand long periods without water, and pelargoniums have adopted a number of different ways to overcome this problem. Some species have evolved swollen stems or roots for water storage; others develop very long roots that can reach subterranean water supplies several metres below the soil surface. Because of the relative scarcity of plant life in these areas the soil is always lacking in humus, and is usually open in texture and well drained. Some species grow directly in beds of gravel. In low rainfall areas plants receive long periods of strong sunshine as there are few clouds. With the exception of *P. endlicherianum* all the species live in regions that are substantially free from frost.

The conditions under which the species live are a good guide to the cultural requirements of hybrids that are derived from them, so it can be seen that the vast majority of cultivars must be grown in good light in a well-drained soil, and should not be overwatered.

LIGHT

Because pelargoniums need good light, a greenhouse or south-facing conservatory is ideal for their culture; a south-facing windowsill in the home is also suitable. Good growing conditions are most important during the winter months, particularly in areas of poor light. The situation is less critical in warm, sunny climates, where they can be grown in the open without protection. To allow the maximum amount of light to penetrate, the glass in a greenhouse or similar structure must be cleaned regularly, preferably just before the onset of winter. During the summer months, when light levels are much higher, there is less of a problem, and under glass some shading will often be required to prevent plants from becoming scorched. Unless the plants are placed out of doors, in summer they must be protected from excessive heat by means of temporary shading. Plants growing in the open are always subject to free movement of air, and in bright weather natural convection allows hot air to rise away from the plants and cooler air to descend. Even with maximum ventilation the confined space of a greenhouse or conservatory impedes the natural air currents and causes an excessive rise in temperature, with consequent damage to the plants.

Shading can be achieved in a number of different ways. For example, special paints can be applied to the outside of the glass, plastic netting or transclucent sheeting can be draped inside the greenhouse or a series of folding slatted blinds can be fixed to the outside. The special shading paints are the cheapest to use and are available from most garden centres. They are easily applied by brush or spray, and unlike ordinary paints can easily be washed off at the end of the season. The chief disadvantage of this type of shading is that it cannot easily be removed

Opposite: Good drainage and bright sunshine bring out the best in pelargoniums in this eye-catching rooftop display

and replaced if there is a temporary spell of dull weather. However, there is at least one product that incorporates a pigment with a refractive index approximating to that of water. This is nearly transparent when wet, and therefore reduces the density of shading during dull, rainy weather. Shading paints can be bought in a choice of two colours, usually white or green. White offers greater efficiency; green blends in better with garden surroundings.

Green or white plastic film or netting is the next most popular means of creating shade. Both types are made specially for the purpose. In a wooden structure they can be pinned directly onto the inside of the glazing bars, but in a metal greenhouse special fittings are needed. However, if the greenhouse is insulated during the winter by lining the inside with thin polyethylene sheeting, the same fittings can normally be used for both purposes. Obviously plastic sheeting must not be fixed so that it obstructs ventilator openings, and even open mesh netting drastically reduces their efficiency.

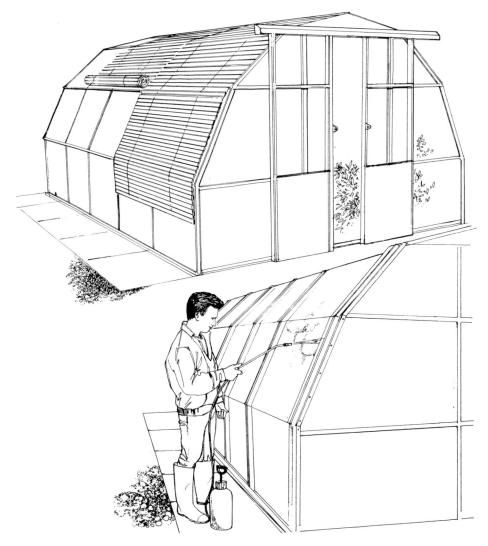

In summer, small greenhouses should be shaded to prevent excessive temperature rises. Slatted blinds (top) are the best method, but shading paints are easily applied and can be washed off at the end of the season

By far the best method of shading is to use slatted roll-up blinds placed over the outside of the greenhouse so the glass itself is prevented from getting hot and there is less heat conduction to the interior. The blinds are easily rolled up or down to maintain a constant light level, but unfortunately are expensive to buy.

The various groups of pelargoniums differ slightly in their requirements for light. Ivy leaf pelargoniums need the maximum amount of available light; at the other extreme are regal pelargoniums, which always require shading from strong sunlight, particularly when they are in flower. Many zonal pelargonium flowers will also last longer if the plants are lightly shaded.

TEMPERATURE

Light and temperature are inextricably linked together, and shading is often required not to reduce the light level but to minimize the effects of excessive heat. The temperature in a greenhouse is dictated both by the efficiency of the ventilators and by the amount of shade provided. In very hot weather even a well-designed house, particularly if it is small in size, will become very hot, and if the temperature consistently rises to over 27°C (80°F) many pelargoniums will begin to suffer. Damage can be prevented by spraying the floor and surroundings with water to create a humid atmosphere; this operation should be carried out in the first half of the day so that excess moisture will have evaporated before the temperature starts to drop at night.

In cold climates the minimum winter temperature is determined by the setting of the heater, and a good level to aim at is about 7.5°C (45°F). Most pelargoniums will be happy at this temperature, but although many of the more sensitive species and cultivars, such as *P. crispum*, 'Mabel Grey' and the tricolour group of zonal pelargoniums, will tolerate this level, losses will be noticeably fewer if the temperature is kept at a minimum of 10°C (50°F). Many of the stronger-growing green-leaved and even bicoloured leaf plants, such as 'Caroline Schmidt', will survive temperatures near to freezing point or even below for short periods, provided that they are kept rather dry at the roots.

Regal pelargoniums particularly resent high temperatures, and they are best kept at temperatures between 7.5°C (45°F) and 16°C (60°F), especially when they are forming flower buds. At higher temperatures they tend to stop growing, and become more open and less bushy in habit. Minimum winter temperatures for this group should not be less than about 4.5°C (40°F).

All miniature forms, particularly miniature zonal pelargoniums, are better kept in a house heated to a minimum of 10°C (50°F) as they are somewhat more delicate than their larger-growing counterparts.

The minimum temperature that plants will tolerate depends largely on their maturity, how much water they are being given and the humidity of the air. Very often a particular minimum temperature is maintained to control the relative humidity and prevent the buildup of potentially lethal fungal diseases such as botrytis. The winter minimum temperature is often dictated not by the inherent sensitivity of the plant to cold but rather to discourage the formation of diseases that are produced by cold, moist air. Pelargoniums will often tolerate slightly lower temperatures than those quoted as long as the atmosphere is dry. (See also page 53.)

HUMIDITY

The atmosphere contains water in the form of vapour, and if the temperature falls it becomes relatively more humid until saturation point is reached and the water condenses out as droplets. Conversely, as the temperature rises and unless there is more water available to evaporate into the atmosphere, the air will become progressively drier. Excessively dry air is very detrimental to plants and open flowers, so on hot days the greenhouse pathways and the floor should be sprayed with water to increase humidity. It is unfortunate that on cool, cloudy days when temperatures stay low, high humidity also damages open flowers by causing them to rot. The skilful grower anticipates these problems, and 'damps down' early on hot days to maintain a suitable level of humidity, allowing the atmosphere to become drier later in the day to anticipate a night-time fall in temperature and the possibility of the next day being cool and wet. Sometimes, usually in winter, it is necessary to lower atmospheric humidity by heating the air to prevent a buildup of fungal diseases. Ivy leaf pelargoniums will also become prone to a physiological disorder called oedema (see page 85) if they are grown in a humid atmosphere.

In a greenhouse it is generally possible to increase the humidity as required. If the plants are growing in a conservatory attached to a house it is not always possible to increase humidity by spraying the floor with water. A compromise solution sometimes has to be made by increasing the level of shading to lower the internal temperature, and increase the relative humidity by this means instead.

Opposite: A fine show of mixed pelargoniums in a conservatory

Left: 'Monkwood Rhapsody' (see page 97), like all regal pelargoniums, resents very high temperatures

In hot dry weather pathways should be damped down to increase atmospheric humidity in the greenhouse

WATERING

The species from which most of the cultivated hybrids have been bred belong to the group that has long, penetrating roots to seek out moisture deep underground. In the confined space of a small pot these roots are unnaturally restricted, so frequent watering is required in hot weather. If by accident the plants are allowed to get too dry the lower leaves will turn yellow and fall off. On the other hand, pelargoniums will not tolerate a waterlogged soil for long; in these circumstances the roots usually decay and the entire plant dies.

Amateur growers usually water their plants individually, or by spraying water over the tops of the plants with a hosepipe. The latter method can be used when the plants are small, but to prevent certain damage its use has to be discontinued in the winter months or when the plants come into flower. Watering each pot individually gives good results, but with a large collection it can be very laborious. A great deal of time can be saved by growing the plants on a specially manufactured absorbent cloth, and allowing the water to rise up from it into the compost by capillary action. This cloth, or capillary matting as it is properly called, is designed to hold enough water to supply the needs of the plants throughout the day. It is woven from synthetic fibres to withstand constant wetness without decay. The matting can be purchased via mail order dealers or from many large garden centres. An underlay of polyethylene sheeting is required, but the benching does not have to be completely flat as water that collects in minor depressions will be redistributed by the absorbent nature of the matting.

To some extent this method of irrigation evens out variations in the water requirement of plants at different stages of growth and in pots of different sizes. Each plant is in contact with all the others via the matting, and if one takes up more water than its neighbour moisture will flow towards it from wetter parts, and vice versa. Although there is thus in effect an automatic redistribution of water between the soil of nearby plants, it should not be completely relied upon – newly potted plants still need to be watered carefully. Water can be allowed to spread across the matting by applying it with a hosepipe at a few strategic points, or via a perforated distribution pipe. The latter method has the advantage that if the pipe is connected to a header tank or cistern an electric sensor can be employed to turn on the water supply automatically when the matting begins to dry out. Small areas of matting can be kept moist by allowing part of it to dip into a trough or cistern that is automatically filled from the mains water supply.

Capillary action will only raise water to a certain height, so it restricts the use of this method to watering standard depth pots of less than 13 to 15 cm (5 to 6 in) in diameter, though the type of compost used and how well it is firmed in the pot also needs to be taken into account.

Pelargoniums should never be grown so close together as to impede the air flow around them or fungal diseases will be encouraged. This is particularly important when using capillary matting because the whole of the benching around the plants is constantly moist. In winter it is better to discontinue the use of capillary matting and to water by hand, so a drier atmosphere can be maintained.

Because it is constantly kept moist, capillary matting quickly becomes fouled by the growth of algae and slime moulds. These are not necessarily harmful, but because they look unsightly they should be kept in check by using an algicide that has been specially developed for the purpose. These are normally obtainable from the matting suppliers. A further interesting alternative is to cover the matting with black polythene sheet that has been regularly perforated with holes (paper-punch size). Provided that there is at least one hole under each pot this system works surprisingly well, although an algicide is still necessary to prevent the formation of slime moulds and bacteria that grow in the dark.

To be able to supply the compost with moisture, the capillary matting must be in contact with it through the drainage holes at the bottom of the pot. Compost in a plastic pot will take up moisture directly from the matting as it does not need to be crocked, but a clay pot will need a wick to lead the water from the matting to the compost. A small strip of matting will make a suitable wick. (Crocking is the term used for putting coarse pieces of material – usually fragments of clay pots – in the bottom of the pot to prevent the compost from falling through the drainage hole at the bottom.)

An alternative approach is to have a small pipe with a metering nozzle leading to each pot so that the plants can be watered individually from a common supply. With this method the plants can be grown on slatted benches, and the air flow between them will be greatly improved. However, if local under- or overwatering is to be avoided the plants all need to be roughly the same size and to grow at the same rate. For this reason this method of watering, known as spaghetti or pot drip irrigation, is used mainly by commercial growers who raise large batches of plants of similar age and size.

In summer the plants need watering whenever the surface of the soil looks and feels dry, and before they start to wilt. As a generalization it is better to keep pelargoniums rather on the dry side than to overwater them. Regal pelargoniums need more water than the others, and the surface of the soil should only just be allowed to dry before watering. On the other hand, ivy leaf pelargoniums and some of the more succulent species, such as *P. tetragonum*, *P. echinatum* and *P. gibbosum*, should be allowed to dry almost completely between each watering or they will become uncharacteristically soft in growth and prone to disease.

Because plants are vulnerable to overwatering when temperatures are low, irrigation should be drastically reduced during the winter months. In hot weather, a well-developed plant in a small pot might need daily watering, but at temperatures below 7.5°C (45°F) it might need only weekly or possibly even monthly watering.

The quality of water used is not critical, and any normal source that is suitable for horticultural purposes will be acceptable. Pelargoniums are tolerant of variations in soil pH (acidity or alkalinity), so the effects of hard or soft water are not particularly pronounced. However, in the long term the most suitable mains water supply is one that is not too hard, i.e. does not contain large quantities of dissolved calcium and magnesium salts. Rainwater can also be used, but it must be stored in clean containers in complete darkness or disease organisms will be able to breed in it and render it unsafe for use.

Ivy leaf pelargoniums planted in a pair of handsome terracotta urns

Regal pelargoniums such as 'Vicky Town' (see page 98) have a very high requirement for potassium

NUTRITION

This section will be of particular interest to potential exhibitors or commercial growers, as it gives detailed information on the particular nutritional requirements of each pelargonium group. Growers who require only a summary of recommendations will find sufficient detail given in the section on feeding on page 47.

It is perhaps surprising that the different groups of pelargoniums require radically different nutrition. This fact also necessitates the use of at least two different feeds, as a compromise produces noticeably inferior results. Regal pelargoniums and the unique group have a very high requirement for potassium (potash), while all the other groups, including zonal and ivy leaf pelargoniums, require more nitrogen than potassium.

In many countries the law requires the analysis of fertilizers to be printed on the packaging. This enables an informed buyer to select the right formulation for a particular purpose. Fertilizers are classified according to the amounts of nitrogen (N), phosphorus (P) and potassium (K) they contain, always given in that order. Instead of quoting the quantity of phosphorus and potassium as a percentage of each element present they are usually expressed as a percentage of their compounds, P_2O_5 and K_2O respectively. The analysis can also be described in terms of a simple ratio, 1:1:1 or 2:1:1 NPK, etc., or as a ratio of the percentages 10:10:10 or 20:10:10 NPK for example.

As an example, the analysis of a fertilizer might be shown on the packet thus:

Nitrogen   10%

Phosphorus as P_2O_5 10%

Potassium as K_2O 27%

This is a 10:10:27 NPK or (approximately) a 1:1:3 formulation. Providing that the manufacturer's instructions for dilution are followed, this should give the same results as a fertilizer having an analysis of 5:5:15 NPK, as it still has the active constituents in the ratio of 1:1:3 NPK. A fertilizer of formulation 1:1:1 or 1:0:1 NPK is said to be balanced because the nitrogen and the potassium content are equal. A high nitrogen fertilizer has more nitrogen than potassium, for example 3:1:1 or 2:1:1 NPK, and a high potassium fertilizer has a higher proportion of potassium than nitrogen, for example a 1:1:3 or 1:1:2 NPK formulation. The only elements that are normally adjusted relative to each other are nitrogen and potassium. Nitrogen encourages large, soft, leafy growth, and potassium creates harder, more disease-resistant growth and improves the colour and quality of fruit and flowers.

This is of course a simplified explanation, as it assumes that all the active ingredients are immediately available to the plant. Some materials, for example John Innes base fertilizer, contain nitrogen in the form of hoof and horn meal. This substance is a mixture of organic compounds that cannot be used directly by the plant; it is necessary for soil bacteria to break them down into simple inorganic compounds before they can be absorbed by the plant roots. Although chemical analysis shows that John Innes base fertilizer contains nitrogen, phosphorus and potassium, it initially behaves as though there were little nitrogen present as only the other two constituents are immediately available to the plants. However, with the exception of those that contain urea, the ingredients of most fertilizers used for liquid feeding are in a form that plants can use immediately.

Light can also affect nutrient requirements; a plant showing slight nitrogen deficiency will recover and grow more strongly if slightly shaded, and will again show nitrogen starvation if replaced in full light. Therefore a plant that looks green and healthy in winter might look pale and starved if given the same fertilizer in summer. Plants therefore need a fertilizer that contains slightly more nitrogen in summer than in winter.

The fertilizer content of potting soil will become unbalanced if plants are overwatered and the excess liquid allowed to run away. Nitrogen, in the form of nitrates, is most easily leached out in this manner, followed by potassium and phosphorus. Phosphorus is more strongly retained if the water supply is hard. Where this occurs it is sometimes unnecessary to feed extra phosphorus, and a 1:0:1 or 1:0:2 NPK fertilizer can be used.

In addition to these three major nutrients, all plants require quantities of calcium, magnesium and sulphur, and much smaller amounts of micronutrients (trace elements), which include boron, iron, manganese, copper, zinc and molybdenum. All of these elements are included in most proprietary liquid feeds.

Many growers do not realize that it is not always the absolute concentration of each individual nutrient that is important but the ratio of the concentrations between various nutrients. For example, even though there might be a normal quantity of magnesium present in the soil, a plant may become deficient in this element if it is fed too much potassium.

Regal pelargoniums

Experience, coupled with soil and leaf analysis, has shown that these plants require relatively high levels of potassium or the flowers will be of poor quality and easily damaged by periods of damp or of bright sunshine. A fertilizer of 1:0:2 or 1:1:2 NPK is suitable for regular use, winter and summer, but if the potassium level is thought to be low a 1:0:3 NPK fertilizer can occasionally be used. Fertilizers that are formulated for feeding tomatoes are also ideal for feeding regal pelargoniums. Regular use of a 1:1:3 or 1:0:3 NPK fertilizer will almost certainly induce magnesium deficiency in some cultivars. Magnesium deficiency causes the area between the leaf veins to become pale green or yellow, and in severe cases large areas of the leaf become brown and die. This disorder is cured by spraying the plants with a solution of Epsom salts (magnesium sulphate) dissolved in water at a rate of 25 g per 25 litres (1 oz per 40 pints) of water, and by changing the feed to a formulation with a lower potassium content.

Plants that have not been potted into fresh compost for some time but have been sustained by liquid feeding are sometimes prone to developing boron deficiency. Boron deficiency is characterized by longitudinal splitting of the petiole (leaf stalk), and minute light brown spotting on the upper surface of the leaves. Sometimes the main veins of the leaves also show brown splitting. In severe cases the stems are swollen and cracked, particularly around the nodes, and when this area is cut open brown, hollow cavities are found. If the plants are examined early in the morning after being well watered the previous evening, the underside of the lower leaves will have a water-soaked appearance. This condition is rare; it is made worse by high soil pH (alkalinity), and mild symptoms are occasionally seen in hard-water areas. Plants with boron deficiency can be cured by watering them once or twice with a solution containing 2.4 ml (12 drops) of borax concentrate in 4.5 l (1 gal) of water. The borax concentrate is made by dissolving 25 g (1 oz) of borax ($Na_2B_4O_7.10H_2O$) in 4.5 l (1 gal) of water. Although small quantities of boron are essential for plant growth larger amounts are poisonous, and as there is little margin for error the deficiency must be carefully diagnosed and treated.

Zonal and ivy leaf pelargoniums

Both these groups require more nitrogen and less potassium than regal pelargoniums. A tomato fertilizer, as recommended for regal pelargoniums, would produce a slightly yellowed appearance, with some of the older leaves becoming tinged with red. A general feed containing 1:1:1 NPK, replaced by an occasional (about one in five) 2:1:1 NPK feed, gives good results. Cultivars with yellow/gold or tricoloured leaves are an exception, and these plants should, like regal pelargoniums, be fed with a high potassium fertilizer. This ensures that the leaves remain brightly coloured and do not take on an overall greenish tinge.

Some growers recommend regular spraying with Epsom salts (magnesium sulphate) to improve the leaf colour of plants. If this treatment is found to be necessary it is probable that mild magnesium deficiency is being induced by using a fertilizer containing too much potassium.

Unlike most zonal pelargoniums those with gold or tricolored leaves require a high potassium feed. Seen here are, on the right, 'Turkish Delight' (see page 110) and, on the opposite page, 'Golden Crest'

FEEDING

When a plant is first potted up the compost contains sufficient nutrients to sustain healthy growth without the need for supplementary feeding; the period that elapses before feeding is started depends on the type of compost used. A John Innes or other soil-based compost usually has a high reserve of nutrients, and plants growing in them do not need to be fed as soon as those in soilless composts. If the plants are in active growth, feeding should begin about 10–12 weeks after potting for soil-based composts, and 4–6 weeks for soilless composts.

When the plants are well established in their pots they should be fed at approximately every fifth watering, i.e. if the plants need watering every day they should be fed every five days, and if they need watering once a week they should be fed every five weeks. This recommendation only applies to liquid feeding; follow the manufacturer's recommendations for other types of product. Alternatives to liquid feeding can consist of top dressing the compost with a solid fertilizer similar to that used in its preparation, or by using fertilizer tablets or spikes that are pushed into the soil or mats that are placed under the plant. Liquid feeding is the most versatile method, as the rate and type of feed can be changed to suit the differing needs of the plant at various stages of its growth or to compensate for variations caused by seasonal fluctuations.

It is essential to use a high potassium feed for regal pelargoniums and for zonal

'Golden Crest' (see page 104)

pelargoniums with gold or tricoloured leaves. A feed that is formulated for tomatoes is suitable and can be used all the year round. With the above exceptions zonal pelargoniums should be fed with a balanced fertilizer, i.e. one containing approximately equal amounts of nitrogen and potassium. Check for yourself the detailed analysis on the package; garden centre assistants will probably have little specialist knowledge of plant nutrition.

Always follow the manufacturer's instructions for the rate of dilution very carefully; if the fertilizer is used too frequently or at the wrong strength, growth will be impaired or the plants may die.

COMPOSTS

Potting composts can be divided into two main types – those that contain a proportion of soil and those that do not. The latter types are usually based on peat, but sometimes pulverized bark, vermiculite, perlite or rockwool are used.

Although they were originally developed in the 1930s, the soil-based John Innes composts still have their advocates. Good quality loam is the most important ingredient. Unfortunately, even with great care in selection, consistent batches of the product are hard to find, and the subsequent growth of plants is unpredictable. On the other hand, peat is a very consistent product and soilless composts usually give reproducible results from bag to bag and from year to year. Commercial growers generally use soilless composts for this reason, and also because they are easier to make than soil-based products. A major advantage of soil-based over soilless composts is that there is nearly always a greater reserve of nutrients; feeding plants is less critical, and they do not need feeding as soon after being repotted.

Peat-based potting composts retain more water than do soil-based types, so it is easy to overwater, particularly in winter. This problem is considerably alleviated by mixing about five volumes of the peat-based compost with one part of coarse grit. This material must be suitable for horticultural use; material bought from a builders' merchant might contain salt or too much chalk. A similar quantity of horticultural perlite can alternatively be used. Products that already contain sand or grit will not need any more to be added.

Some growers mix soil-based and soilless composts together to try to obtain some of the advantages of both products, and to a certain extent this works; many commercial growers add a portion of steamed (partially sterilized) loam to a fertilized peat and sand mixture. However, as John Innes composts are a mixture of sterilized loam, peat and sand the difference is hard to determine. Some authorities warn of chemical reactions that may be caused by mixing different types of compost together, but there is no scientific basis for these statements. However, ammonia gas can be released if chalk, limestone, dolomite or magnesian limestone are mixed with other chemicals used in the preparation of composts. They are safe if they are added separately to soil or peat during the preparation of compost.

Many growers will buy small quantities of ready-mixed composts from a garden centre, but quite large savings can be made by mixing them at home. The easiest way is to buy a kit of chemicals and mix it with a suitably sized bale of peat. Provided that the instructions are followed carefully the product will be equivalent to a good quality, commercially made product. John Innes composts are much more difficult to make as the loam must be partially sterilized by steam at a carefully controlled temperature; this process requires specialized equipment that is expensive to buy and operate.

Some composts now contain slow-release fertilizers; these are small beads of fertilizer that have been given a thin resin coating to slow down and control the availability of the nutrients. Much larger quantities of fertilizer can be incorporated into the compost at the time of manufacture without any risk of damage due to overfeeding. The special nature of the resin coating ensures that the nutrients are released at a controlled rate that depends largely on temperature and not on other factors such as soil pH or moisture content. Composts containing these fertilizers work well, and depending on the type of product used can feed plants for up to nine months.

POTTING, RE-POTTING AND POTTING ON

These important procedures must not be confused, as they refer to distinctly different operations performed for different purposes. Potting or potting-up consists of planting a young cutting or an established plant from a bed into a pot for the first time. Re-potting is the process in which old soil is removed from the roots of a plant before it is potted into, normally, the same size pot or one that is slightly smaller; the latter process is sometimes called potting back. Re-potting is usually performed on an old plant that has been in the same pot for a considerable period, or occasionally on a young plant that is suspected of having a root problem. Potting-on is the process of putting a healthy, actively growing plant into a larger container without disturbing the roots, so that growth can continue without a check.

Pot up rooted cuttings as soon as the root system is well established to prevent any check to growth

When a young plant has filled the compost with roots it is time to pot on into a larger container

A cutting should be potted up as soon as it is well rooted. Delay usually means that the root system becomes so extensive that damage to it is inevitable, causing a check to growth. Cuttings that have been rooted in peat blocks or small individual containers can be potted up at a much later stage without root damage, but the process should not be delayed for too long or the nutrients in the compost will become exhausted, and again a check to growth will result.

Do not plant a rooted cutting into a large container straight away or the soil will become sour before the roots are able to grow into it. An 8 or 9 cm (3 or $3\frac{1}{2}$ in) container is quite adequate for potting up an average-sized pelargonium cutting; those of miniature cultivars are best confined to even smaller pots.

The potting compost should not be pressed down hard with the fingers; only very light pressure is needed. A good method is to pour the compost around the plant and settle it down by slapping the side of the pot or by tapping it sharply several times onto the potting bench. Over-firming must be avoided as it reduces the size of the air spaces in the compost, making it more liable to waterlogging and consequent sourness.

When the young plant has filled the compost with roots it is time to pot on into a larger container. If this is done too early there is a risk that the plant will fail to establish because the soil has become sour; if it is left too late the plant may be slow to grow away because the growth has become hard and checked. If plastic pots have been used, the soil ball can be carefully knocked out and the state of root development inspected directly and, if necessary, the pot replaced without damage. This is not so easy to achieve with clay pots, as the surface is rougher and some root damage is inevitable. If for some reason a plant cannot be potted on at the correct time it should be fed to prevent a check to growth.

Plants should be potted on when necessary into larger containers until the pots are big enough to sustain them for the rest of the growing season. The final size of pot will vary greatly depending on the type of plant being grown. For example, some miniature zonal pelargoniums will not need anything larger than a 6.5 to 8 cm ($2\frac{1}{2}$ to 3 in) pot, whereas a large-sized zonal pelargonium will need a 20 cm (8 in) pot to reach full maturity. A good-sized regal pelargonium may need a 30 cm (12 in) pot in its second season. It is an important part of the grower's skill to be able to decide exactly which size pot a plant needs and when it should be potted on. This skill is only learned by experience, and there are no short cuts.

It is best to re-pot one-year-old plants when rapid growth starts at the beginning of the second season. The exact timing of this will depend on the weather and on the temperature being maintained inside the greenhouse. Some growers do not re-pot their plants every year but prefer to sustain them by top dressing the old compost with a solid fertilizer or by liquid feeding. This method works well with soil-based composts as they have the ability to hold a large reserve of nutrients, but the author prefers annual re-potting of all plants growing in soilless composts.

Re-potting must be done carefully; the old compost must be removed by squeezing the soil ball with the fingers until it breaks up and then by carefully shaking the remainder away. There is always a risk of damaging the roots at this stage, and the shock to the plants can be lessened by pruning the plant stems back at the same time. This will help to maintain the natural balance between the roots and the aerial portions of the plant. (See also pruning and shaping, page 56.)

Opposite: Mixed pelargoniums: in the foreground 'Lilac Gem'; behind, from left to right, are 'Spitfire', 'Deacon Lilac Mist' and 'Golden Crest', with 'Patchwork Quilt' at the back

In addition to taking up mineral salts and water, plant roots also release substances into the soil; it is well established that roses will not grow in the same place indefinitely or a general decline in their condition is inevitable.

It is probably for this reason that changing the soil around the roots of a pot-grown plant is more effective in stimulating growth than just adding more fertilizer. Provided that re-potting is done with care losses should be minimal, and the revitalizing effect on the plants is well worth the effort involved.

The choice between clay or plastic pots is a matter of personal preference; some growers still consider that they get better results by using the traditional clay pots. However, with some modifications in cultural techniques plastic pots will give equally good results. The changes are necessary because of the different properties of the two materials from which the pots are made. Clay is porous and allows air and moisture to pass through it easily, while plastic pots are completely impervious. Plants growing in clay pots ideally need a compost that is retentive of moisture, but those growing in plastic pots need a well-draining compost because they are more likely to be overwatered.

OVERWINTERING

Pelargoniums need protection from frost, and in areas where freezing conditions exist they must be given some form of shelter. The ideal solution is to keep the collection in a greenhouse, but a south-facing conservatory is equally good. It is not important whether the greenhouse is constructed of wood or metal, but as metal greenhouses usually have narrower glazing bars, they admit more light and this can make a slight difference to the quality of winter growth. A greenhouse must be situated where it receives the maximum amount of available light, and there should be no major obstructions near it that can cast shadows. This is fundamental to good culture, and it is worth remembering that an object that does not cause an obstruction in summer could well cast a dense shadow onto the greenhouse in winter when the sun is lower in the sky. On the other

Slatted benches allow free circulation of air and are a great help in pelargonium cultivation

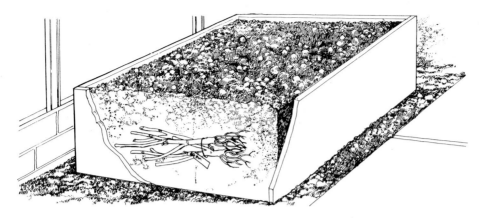

If no better method is available pelargoniums can be cut back and overwintered in a protected 'clamp' (see page 54 for further details)

hand, if the site is very exposed a compromise might have to be made to give the greenhouse shelter from potentially damaging winds.

Because pelargoniums dislike still, damp conditions it is a good idea to equip the greenhouse with slatted benches to allow air to circulate freely around the plants. These are quite easy to construct, and if the slats are laid loosely over a wooden framework they can be adjusted to suit the requirements of differently sized plants. All wooden surfaces should be liberally painted with a suitable preservative approved for horticultural use. Ordinary wood preservatives, especially creosote, give off fumes that can kill plants, so these products must never be used inside a greenhouse. Another suitable form of benching can be made from galvanized metal mesh laid over a supporting framework of wood or bricks.

In theory any form of approved greenhouse heating apparatus can be used. In practice, because pelargoniums are damaged by excess humidity some forms of heating are more suitable than others. When paraffin (kerosene) is burnt, approximately 14 parts by weight produces 18 parts by weight of water, so greenhouse heaters that use this fuel cannot maintain a dry atmosphere. This is also true of many propane- or butane-fired gas heaters. These problems do not occur with the more complex and expensive oil- or gas-fired heaters used by commercial growers. These have a heat exchanger that allows moisture and combustion gases to be vented directly to the outside, so that only warm, dry air is circulated within the greenhouse. For an amateur grower the most satisfactory means of heating is by an electric fan heater, as this has the added advantage of creating a forced circulation of air. Unlike other systems that give off water, electric heating lowers the relative humidity of the air, and as already explained this can make a slightly lower than normal minimum temperature acceptable. With the help of an accurate thermostat it is easier to maintain precise control of the level of electric heating than with most other systems. Both these advantages can lead to quite large savings, which will often more than offset the initially higher cost of using electricity as a fuel. Whichever system is used, a further saving in cost can be made by insulating the greenhouse with thin, clear, polyethylene sheeting. For best effect a small gap of at least 1 cm ($\frac{1}{2}$ in) should be left between the insulating film and the inside of the glass. In wooden greenhouses the insulation can be pinned directly to the inside of the glazing bars, but special fittings are needed for metal greenhouses.

It is easy to see that the heater is maintaining the required temperature during the day, but few growers bother to check the temperature in their greenhouse in the small hours of a cold winter night. The easiest way to check that the heating system is working properly is to use a maximum–minimum recording thermometer. These instruments are quite cheap, and show the highest and lowest temperatures recorded since the instrument was last set. A recording thermometer is an essential piece of equipment that could pay for itself many times over.

If a heated greenhouse or conservatory is not available it is still possible to house a small collection of plants on a windowsill indoors. A south-facing window is suitable but it is unlikely that large plants can be accommodated in this way. An alternative approach is to insulate the plants for the coldest part of the winter by burying them in nearly dry peat. Plants growing outside should be left for as long as possible before being lifted and at least half the length of each stem pruned back. All soft wood and the majority of the leaves must be removed, and most of the soil should be shaken from the roots. The plants are immersed in a suspension of a fungicide containing benomyl, made up at the usual strength for spraying, then allowed to drain and dry for 24 hours. After this they are bundled together and buried to a minimum depth of 15 cm (6 in) in nearly dry peat. A

Plants growing outside should be left for as long as possible before lifting and pruning back

'Alex' (see page 100) is easy to grow and will thrive on a south-facing windowsill. It is also excellent for bedding out

similar layer of peat should be placed under the plants so that they are raised above the level of the ground. In exceptionally cold conditions it may be necessary to place sacking or other similar material over the top of the heap. The plants can be stored by this means in an unheated greenhouse, shed, garage or any other unheated outhouse where they will be protected from rain. The storage area can even be built out of doors as long as the layer of peat is built up well above ground level and completely covered with plastic sheeting to prevent water getting in. In early spring the plants should be potted up and stood in an unheated greenhouse or conservatory. Covering the plants with newspaper on cold nights prevents them from being damaged by late frosts. Tests conducted with beginners has shown that this method can be quite successful, and on average only about one plant in twelve is lost.

This method is not meant to act as a substitute for a heated greenhouse; while the plants are buried the owner will not be able to enjoy the winter flowers that are produced in a more suitable environment, and if the plants start to rot or deteriorate in storage nothing will be known until the spring, when it might be too late to save them. It is, however, a useful method for keeping plants alive that would otherwise have to be discarded because of lack of space. It can also be used as a temporary measure in cold weather while a greenhouse is being constructed.

Almost all pelargoniums benefit from occasional pruning; this may consist of simply removing the growing tip or, on an established plant, removal of up to two thirds of each stem

PRUNING AND SHAPING

All pelargoniums are improved as pot plants by a certain amount of pruning and shaping. As they are very diverse in their habit of growth, size and vigour it is difficult to make a broad recommendation that covers all groups in every situation. A distinction can be made between the annual process of hard pruning or major reshaping between each growing season, and the more frequent removal of the growing tips during the main growth period.

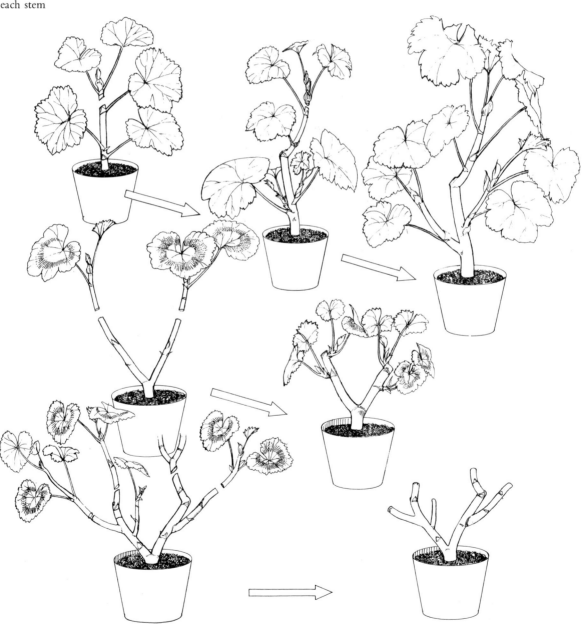

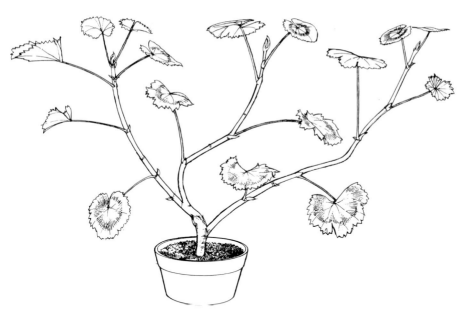

The appearance of leggy plants can be greatly improved by hard pruning. This will encourage the formation of new growth on the lower parts of the stem

Many pelargoniums should have their growing tip pinched out at the same time or very soon after they are first potted up. At this stage the plants will probably have only two or three pairs of leaves and, on average, be no more than 5 to 8 cm (2 to 3 in) high. Many zonal pelargoniums, particularly the older cultivars, will grow as a single leg if they are not pinched at an early stage. Many of the scented leaf plants will benefit greatly from early pinching, or stopping as it is sometimes called. This process should be repeated on subsequent growth as many times as is necessary to form a shapely plant. However, because pinching also delays blooming the procedure should be kept to a minimum so that there is a reasonable flowering period.

Not all pelargoniums should be pinched; many, such as 'Morval' and most of the Deacon series, will naturally form neat-looking, dome-shaped plants, and stopping will give them an ugly, flattened appearance. Most modern regal pelargoniums and miniature and dwarf zonal pelargoniums should not be stopped, though some benefit from an occasional pinch during later growth.

It is obviously difficult for a beginner to decide which cultivars should be pinched, and if there is any doubt, stopping should be delayed until there are clear signs that a plant is only producing one or two main stems.

In recent years chemical growth regulation has become possible, and this method is now frequently used by the majority of large commercial growers. The substance currently favoured for this purpose is called cycocel. It is very effective but also very poisonous, and particularly harmful if splashed into the eyes or on other delicate parts of the body. Unlike pinching, cycocel stimulates growth from all the leaf axils, not just the uppermost ones, and it also reduces the distance between leaf nodes. Although the effect soon wears off, a plant that has been treated with cycocel will have more stems and produce more flowers than one that has only been stopped. Because of its dangerous nature the sale of cycocel is in some countries limited to recognized commercial growers, and is not available to the general public.

If a plant has been overlooked at an earlier stage, much more drastic treatment than pinching out the tips of the stems may be necessary. When plants have been neglected in this way they often lose their lower leaves and their appearance is said to be 'leggy'. These plants can be severely pruned by removing up to three-quarters of each stem, which will encourage new growth to be made low down and overcome the problem of legginess. To avoid crushing and bruising the stems all pruning of mature wood should be carried out with sharp secateurs. The cuts must be made just above a node or the stems are likely to rot.

After taking cuttings for the following season some growers dispose of the old plants at the end of the summer. This is often a forced choice, as it can be costly to overwinter large plants because they take up a great deal of heated space. However, some pelargoniums, particularly regal pelargoniums, are better if they can be kept for a second or third season. Towards the end of the summer these plants should be pruned back quite hard by cutting off half to two-thirds of each stem. This is also a good opportunity to prune any plants that need reshaping, and at the same time reduces the amount of greenhouse space required by each plant. Many zonal and scented leaf pelargoniums also benefit from this treatment, but other plants such as 'Morval', 'Deacon Lilac Mist', 'Vina', 'Turkish Delight', etc. only need light pruning as they are naturally dwarf-growing and very bushy. These cultivars can still be improved by pruning away weak or old stems, but they should not be subjected to the harsh treatment needed by more rampant types.

If it becomes necessary hard pruning can be carried out at most times of the year, but to avoid stem rot and other subsequent damage it is advisable not to prune the plants during late autumn, winter or early spring. Even at other times of the year it is a good idea to dust the cut surfaces with flowers of sulphur to prevent them from becoming infected. After the plants have been pruned it is a good time to re-pot them using fresh compost; they can be put back into the same sized pot, or preferably a slightly smaller one. The plants should then be able to fill the pots with fresh roots before growth stops in winter, and in the following spring it will be easier to sustain growth by potting on again into a larger container.

GROWING STANDARDS AND GRAFTING

A standard is a plant shaped rather like a small tree, which has been trained to grow as a single straight stem before being allowed to form a bushy head. All types of pelargonium can be grown in this way, though some groups, such as modern regal pelargoniums, are much more difficult than others. Zonal pelargoniums or ivy leaf pelargoniums are the easiest to train, and beginners would be well advised to start with one of these. (For recommendations, see the tables on page 116.)

A standard is grown by pinching out all the existing and subsequent side shoots from a young cutting as soon as they are large enough to handle. The stem is kept straight by being tied every 10 cm (4 in) to a bamboo cane. All the leaves attached to the main stem are retained for as long as possible or the plant will stop growing. Once the plant has nearly reached the required height the growing tip should be pinched out and the side shoots from the top three nodes left to grow.

'Hazel Perfection'
(see page 96)
grown as a
standard. Regal
pelargoniums are
not easy to grow
in ths way but, as
can be seen, the
result is spectacular
and well worth the
effort

These side branches are the nucleus of the head, and they should have their tips pinched out as necessary to encourage bushiness.

A vigorous cultivar that does not branch readily is easy to train as a single stem but is difficult to form into a bushy head, and vice versa. One solution to this problem is to spray a young cutting of a reasonably bushy cultivar, such as 'Deacon Bonanza', with a solution of gibberelic acid. This considerably increases the distance between each pair of leaves (the internodal length) and reduces the time taken to grow it to the required height. When the effect of the spray wears off the plant will naturally form a bushy head. Some specialist nurseries can supply gibberelic acid for this purpose and instructions for its use, but generally the substance is difficult to obtain.

An alternative approach is to use the technique of grafting; a stock (rootstock) is chosen that is easy to train as a single stem, and on top of this is grafted a different cultivar (the scion) that naturally forms a bushy head.

Zonal and ivy leaf pelargoniums can both be grafted satisfactorily onto zonal pelargonium rootstocks. Regal pelargoniums can also be grafted onto the same stock, but they do not thrive and are better grafted onto one of the unique group. Any vigorous zonal pelargonium can, at least in theory, be used as a rootstock; 'Caroline Schmidt' has been used by the author for many years with very good results. This rootstock happily accepts zonal, miniature, dwarf zonal and ivy leaf pelargoniums. Regal pelargoniums grow best on a scented leaf pelargonium stock such as *P. graveolens* or on a unique such as 'Paton's Unique'. The latter is probably the best choice, as *P. graveolens* tends to produce a lot of sucker growth from the roots.

A standard can be grown by training a cutting as a single stem before it is allowed to form a bushy head. **1.** Remove all side shoots and flower buds; **2.** Remove the growing tip when the stem has reached the required height; **3.** Encourage a bushy head to develop

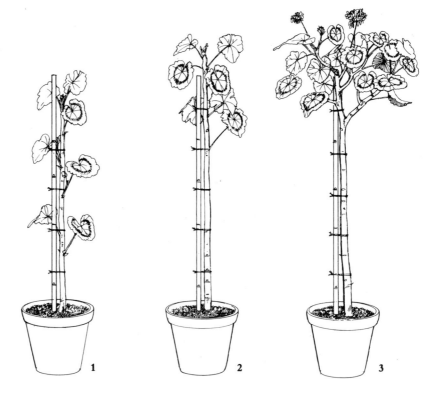

Growing a good standard can take as long as two years, so there is no point in slowing down the process further by starting with inferior material. A number of healthy cuttings of the selected rootstock should be taken, and only the most vigorous ones potted up for growing on. To obtain the straightest stems, cuttings should be taken early in the year so that their growth can be completed within one growing season.

As soon as practicable the plant should be tied to a small bamboo cane, and retied approximately every 10 cm (4 in) to keep the stem straight. All side shoots and flower buds are removed as soon as they are large enough to handle, but the leaves attached to the main stem must not be removed. Whenever necessary the plants are potted on and the bamboo cane changed for a larger one. They should not be subjected to any check in growth at this stage or the time taken to produce the standard will be greatly increased. When the rootstock has reached the

1 and 2. The scion of one pelargonium can be grafted onto the stock of another using an inverted saddle graft technique; 3. Bind the graft firmly with raffia; 4. Cover the top of the plant with a clear plastic bag

The Harlequin series of ivy leaf pelargoniums have been created by grafting. Shown here, clockwise from the top, are 'Harlequin Picotee', 'Harlequin Rosie O'Day', 'Harlequin Alpine Glow' and 'Harlequin My Love'

required height, and provided that it is at a time of year when the plants are growing vigorously, the graft can be made. The height chosen should be in proportion to the ultimate size of the head. For example, a miniature zonal pelargonium would need to be grafted onto a leg of anything from 25 to 60 cm (10 in to 2 ft), but a full-sized zonal pelargonium would need a rootstock of at least 60 cm (2 ft). A cutting of the scion is then taken; this cutting should be 5 to 8 cm (2 to 3 in) long, and only the lower leaves need be removed. The lower part is cut into a wedge shape with a clean, sharp razor blade or scalpel – an ordinary knife is unlikely to be sharp enough for this particular purpose. Care must be taken to avoid injury; double-edged razor blades are made safer by covering up one edge with adhesive tape. Do not allow the cut surfaces of the scion to dry while the rootstock is being prepared or the graft will probably fail. If necessary dip it into a small jar of clean water while the other work is in progress.

The rootstock should have the tip or the top few centimetres cut off at a point where the stem is approximately the same diameter as the scion, though if a good match cannot be made the graft will probably still succeed. An inverted V-shaped notch is then cut into the top of the stock to match the shape of the prepared scion. The aim is to make the two an exact match so that one fits perfectly into the other, but in practice fairly wide tolerances are acceptable. The scion is then pressed firmly into the stock and the two parts are bound together with garden raffia or twine, using sufficient tension to mould the two halves into intimate contact with each other and to expel as much air as possible from between the cut surfaces. Always bind the stock and scion together with a material that allows air and moisture to penetrate or the wound may rot. Cleanliness is important throughout the procedure, and the hands, tools and worksurfaces must be kept scupulously clean. With a little practice the technique is quickly mastered and it makes the otherwise difficult job of growing tall regal pelargonium standards relatively easy.

When the graft has been completed the top of the plant should be covered with a clear plastic bag, the open end of which is brought together and tied to the stem below the graft union. The plant must be kept shaded. After seven days the lower end of the bag may be opened to allow more air to enter. It is removed completely after another two or three days. Two weeks later, approximately 24 days after the graft was made, the union of the stock and scion will be strong enough to allow the removal of the binding. Subsequent development and training of the head then follows usual procedures.

In normal circumstances the cells of the two different plants that make up the graft do not mix, but occasionally a graft hybrid or chimaera is formed that shows characteristics of both the stock and the scion. The Harlequin series of ivy leaf pelargoniums has been created by a grafting technique, but in this case the transmission of a virus or virus-like organism from 'Rouletta', one of the parents, is thought to be responsible for the dramatic alteration of the resulting plants' characters.

'Rouletta' (see page 114) is responsible for the dramatic flower variation seen in the Harlequin series

EXHIBITING

This can be a useful exercise, for it demonstrates and compares a grower's skill with others, as judged by other experienced growers. Most show plants will have been grown for a year or more, so it is necessary for the intending exhibitor to obtain and study copies of rules and various schedules at least a year before the show date. It will also be a good idea for the aspiring exhibitor to visit as many shows as possible to assess the standard required and to make notes of the cultivars that win prizes. This is a valuable exercise, as some cultivars are very much easier to grow to show standard than others, and no extra allowance will be made by the judges for growing difficult ones. (See the Tables of Recommendations on page 116.) The principles of growing exhibition plants are little different from those for ordinary decoration, but if the highest standards are to be achieved great attention must be paid to every aspect of cultivation.

Assuming that the show is to be held in the summer of the following year, the following paragraphs outline the basic methods used to produce a zonal pelargonium show plant.

A number of healthy cuttings of the selected cultivar or cultivars are rooted, and the best of them are potted up and grown on in 8 to 9 cm (3 to $3\frac{1}{2}$ in) containers. Another selection is made at this stage, and only the very best plants are kept. The number of plants retained depends on the space available, but as disasters often happen (even as late as travelling to the show) there must be an adequate safety allowance. The time for taking cuttings is not critical as growth can be controlled by pruning, but if the class in the show restricts the pot size to 13 cm (5 in), the cuttings should be taken in late summer. If the pot size is not limited, cuttings can be taken to advantage in early spring so that the plants can attain maximum size.

Regular stopping and minor pruning will be needed to encourage bushiness and to form the plants into a rounded dome or ball shape. They will grow towards the direction of maximum light, and it is an essential part of the shaping process to move the plants round a quarter of a turn each week to even out the pattern of growth. Regularly remove all flower buds as they become big enough to handle. This is to prevent the plants from wasting energy producing unwanted flowers that could otherwise be turned into growth.

Keep a sharp lookout for any signs of pests or diseases, and take appropriate action. If the same troubles are experienced every year it is advisable to anticipate the problem and take remedial action before any signs of damage can be seen. From now on the plants should be given every care, and watering, pruning, feeding, potting on and re-potting should be carried out at exactly the right time. The plants must not be checked or allowed to suffer neglect at any stage of their growth.

During the winter the plants should be checked frequently, and dead and yellowing leaves removed. If any signs of damage or rotting of the stems are seen the affected areas should be dusted with flowers of sulphur to prevent it spreading. To make absolutely sure that no harm will come to them, exhibition plants are best overwintered at a slightly higher temperature than the main collection. It is also better to avoid pruning or stopping during the winter as the cut ends of the stems will be liable to rot.

When spring arrives the plants should be re-potted or potted back using fresh compost. Any final shaping should be carried out now, but if the work was carried out properly the previous year little remedial treatment should be needed. However, occasional pinching will still be needed, and the routine of turning the plants must not be neglected. Do not be afraid to use small canes or stakes at any stage of growth to help train the stems in a particular direction; these can be removed at a later date after the growth has hardened and become fixed in the required position. While they are growing the trusses of flowers can also be repositioned for best effect by tying them to short stakes. It will be necessary temporarily to support all the flower trusses of zonal pelargoniums while the plants are being transported to the show.

To allow sufficient time for the plants to come into full flower, stopping must be discontinued at a certain time before the show. This period can range from 15 weeks for some doubles to as little as 10 weeks for single flowered cultivars. All flower buds should be left on from that time, but four weeks before the show all open flowers should be removed, leaving only those that are unopened or just showing colour. Do not attempt to pot on plants after the flower buds have formed, or leafy growth will be encouraged that might hide some of the flowers. Assuming that a dry atmosphere can be maintained, and if the plants are lightly shaded, the open blossom will last for up to two weeks. Pick out dead florets from the flowerheads with a pair of tweezers; if there are still buds left to open, the gaps formed will soon close.

The last two feeds can contain a higher level than usual of potassium (a 1:1:2 or 1:0:2 NPK fertilizer) so that the flower colour is enhanced and growth slightly hardened to help prevent damage during transit. Remember that jolts and vibration will cause petals to fall, especially from the single flowered cultivars, so it is prudent to put some thought into the best way of getting plants to the show in an undamaged condition.

These instructions are for growing normal-sized zonal pelargoniums. They can easily be adapted to the individual needs of other groups if their specialized requirements are thoroughly understood.

Knowledge gained from personal experience is the only sure road to success, and the beginner who grows for exhibition should not be too disheartened if prizes do not come quickly. One final tip is to remember that it is very important to be able to time the plants to be at their peak on the day of the show. It is therefore essential to keep a detailed diary of the dates when procedures such as potting, feeding and final stopping were carried out, so that techniques can gradually be improved and refined.

4
Propagation

The propagation of pelargoniums is not difficult, though the procedures involved are little different from those followed for most other plants. Just after cuttings have been taken, and before roots have formed, it is necessary to keep them in a humid atmosphere or to spray them frequently to prevent excessive wilting. Under these conditions they are prone to damping off and other fungal diseases, so it is necessary to make sure that all tools, equipment, compost, etc. are clean and free from disease organisms. Newly planted cuttings should be protected by watering them in or by spraying them with a suitable fungicide. If these elementary precautions are taken a high percentage of cuttings should root successfully.

The best time to take cuttings is when the plants are actively growing in spring, summer or autumn, but with the right equipment it is possible to propagate pelargoniums at any time of the year.

PROPAGATION FROM CUTTINGS

To prevent a gradual deterioration in quality, cuttings should always be taken from plants that have been selected for the quality of their flowers, for freedom from pests and disease, for their vigour and as good examples of their taxon. Many growers sell or exhibit their best plants and use the rejects for propagation. This is a great mistake, for eventually their undesirable characteristics will, by a process of selection, become more apparent in the offspring.

The easiest time of the year to root pelargonium cuttings is in the period of most active growth, i.e. in early spring and late summer. Late winter or early spring cuttings will become large enough to flower in the same season, and many commercial growers propagate a large proportion of their cuttings at this time. Amateur growers often take cuttings in the late summer or early autumn so that the plants will be well established before colder weather but still be small enough to avoid overcrowding the greenhouse in winter.

Pelargoniums are usually propagated from tip cuttings, i.e. the top 5 to 8 cm (2 to 3 in) of a stem. Cuttings should be taken with a razor blade or very sharp knife, severing it from the main stem just above a leaf node. Instead of taking them with a knife, some growers prefer to break the cuttings off from the mother plant; although in favourable conditions this method will give satisfactory results, in other circumstances it can damage both the mother plant and the cutting. All fully developed leaves should be removed, together with the leaf stipules, and the end of the cutting trimmed to just below a leaf node (see illustration).

It is important to choose the correct place to sever the cutting from the main stem. This is because of the way that pelargoniums stems will sometimes die back to the nearest node after the growing tip has been removed, and although no disease is initially involved infection will often occur, causing the whole of the stem to rot. If the stem is cleanly cut just above a node, die back does not usually

Opposite: Zonal pelargoniums in a mixed display

Take pelargonium cuttings just above a node, remove the lowest leaves and trim to just below a node before inserting into cutting compost (see page 70)

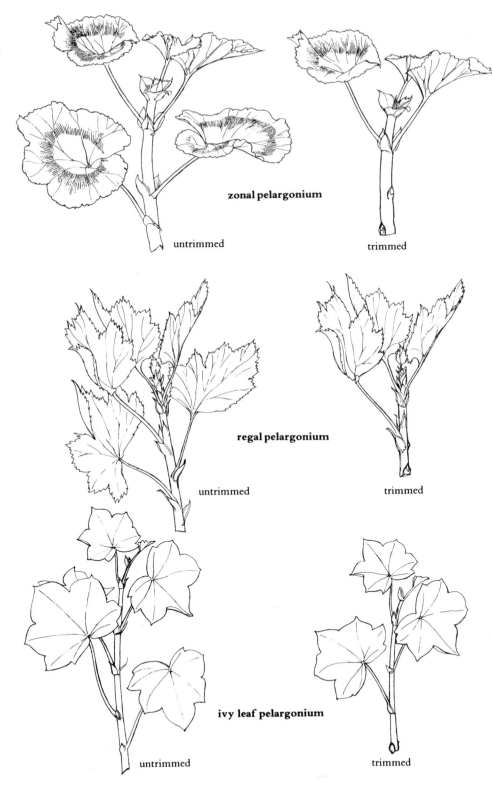

zonal pelargonium

untrimmed

trimmed

regal pelargonium

untrimmed

trimmed

ivy leaf pelargonium

untrimmed

trimmed

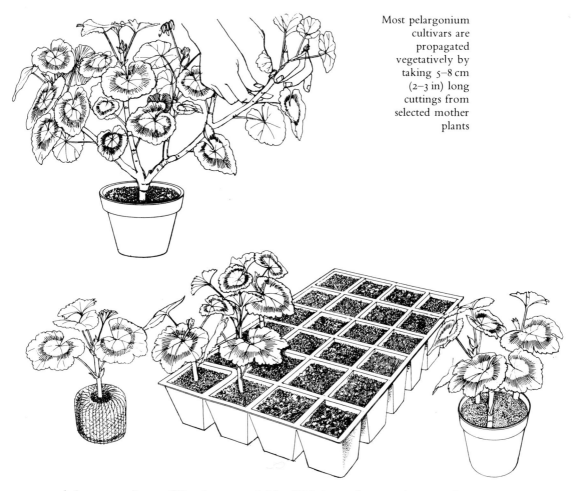

Most pelargonium cultivars are propagated vegetatively by taking 5–8 cm (2–3 in) long cuttings from selected mother plants

Prepared cuttings can be planted in a variety of different containers. (*From left to right*: net-covered peat block, partitioned tray, around the edge of a pot)

occur and the cut surface will heal over quickly. This is another good reason for not breaking cuttings off the plants, as it is much more difficult to predict precisely where the break will occur and there is also a greater risk of bruising the tissues.

Cuttings can be taken in this manner from all *Pelargonium* species and cultivars. Cuttings taken from dwarf and miniature plants will need to be smaller than the size quoted above, but as cuttings with a stem length of 2.5 cm (1 in) or less will be very much more likely to fail, these should be avoided if possible.

Hormone rooting powders or solutions noticeably speed up rooting, but they also produce harmful side-effects on some groups of pelargoniums, and must therefore be used with care. A layer of new tissue grows at the base of a cutting before the new roots emerge. If hormone rooting powder is used the amount of tissue becomes excessively large and cracks open, leading to infection and the subsequent collapse of the plant. At first the cuttings often look very healthy, but they start to wilt and die soon after being potted up. The problem mainly occurs with soft-stemmed cuttings of zonal and ivy leaf pelargoniums, while regal pelargoniums, which root more slowly anyway, are not affected by this problem. Although regal and angel pelargoniums root readily in spring, summer and autumn, some cultivars are almost impossible to root during the winter without the assistance of hormone rooting powder. To get a suitable length of stem many miniature zonal pelargonium cuttings have to be taken with a relatively hard or woody portion at the base. These cuttings will also root more readily and with greater success if treated with hormone rooting powder.

Several cuttings can be inserted round the edge of a pot, or up to forty of them can be planted in a standard seed tray. However, the best method is to plant them singly in partitioned trays or in specially designed, net covered peat blocks. The latter methods allow for easy transplanting with a minimum of root disturbance. Cuttings that have not been planted in separate containers must be potted on as soon as the roots are well formed and before they become tangled together, though despite these precautions some damage will be inevitable.

Depending on their size, cuttings should be planted to a depth of between 1 and 2.5 cm ($\frac{1}{2}$ to 1 in). The compost used should be specially formulated for rooting cuttings or for seed sowing. Do not use ordinary potting compost or garden soil or the results will be very unsatisfactory. A mixture of equal parts of peat and sand or other sterile materials, such as horticultural perlite or vermiculite, can also be used, either alone or mixed with an equal volume of peat. The latter materials contain no nutrients, so to avoid a check in growth it is essential to feed the cuttings as soon as roots start to form. Properly formulated cuttings compost invariably gives the best results, as the type of nutrients and their concentration are adjusted to supply the special needs of a young plant

'Shimmer' (see page 109) is an unusual soft apricot-orange with a silky sheen

while the new root system is forming; ordinary potting composts usually contain a level of fertilizer high enough to inhibit root formation in a cutting or very young seedling.

When the cuttings have been planted they should be watered with a suspension of a fungicide containing benomyl or iprodione made up at the strength recommended by the manufacturers for spraying. Newly planted cuttings should be shaded from strong sunshine to prevent excessive wilting. This is most critical for regal pelargoniums, and in hot weather they will also need regular spraying with clean water, though this must be discontinued approximately 10 days after the date of insertion. Zonal pelargonium cuttings will appreciate a little shade after planting and an occasional spray with water, but ivy leaf pelargoniums, which have better protection against water loss, should not need this treatment.

At a soil temperature of 18°C (64°F) zonal pelargoniums should root in about 10 to 14 days, and should normally be ready for potting in 17 to 21 days. Regal pelargoniums root much more slowly, taking between 20 and 40 days depending on the particular cultivar. On average they take at least 20 to 30 days to root, and the cuttings are not ready for potting until 6 to 8 weeks after insertion.

The young roots produced by cuttings from a modern strain of regal pelargonium cutting are fibrous, almost transparent, and very brittle. A relatively small jolt will detach the entire root system from the base of the now brown and swollen stem. Plants sent by mail order are often subjected to severe shocks in transit, and those who are unfamiliar with this unusual mode of growth sometimes mistakenly believe that they were not rooted when dispatched by the nursery. The older, less compact types of regal pelargonium and members of other groups have a much thicker and more vigorous root system that is clearly visible and less easily damaged. For details of potting up rooted cuttings see page 50 in the chapter on Cultivation.

TISSUE CULTURE

This is a sophisticated laboratory technique beyond the scope of most amateur and many smaller professional growers. Despite this restriction there are interesting implications in the method, which should be understood by all growers. Tissue culture can be used to propagate quickly large numbers of plants from perhaps one small specimen and, at the same time, rid it of disease. Plants are now available from many nurseries and garden centres that have been propagated from virus-free stock produced by this method.

The basic technique used is to cut the tiny growing points (called meristems) from the tips of the stems of selected plants and transfer them to a special sterile growing medium contained in a closed glass vessel. The growing medium is in the form of a clear jelly that contains normal plant nutrients together with sugars and small amounts of particular hormones to regulate growth. The meristems are often less than a millimetre long and the plant material, surroundings, equipment and air have to be sterile to prevent infection.

The hormone levels in the nutrient jelly are initially adjusted to cause the meristem to produce new growing points at a greatly increased rate. At this stage no roots are formed; the young plantlets are grown in chambers lit by artificial lighting and are sustained by the sugars and minerals contained in the jelly. After a few weeks many clusters of tiny plants will have formed; each one can be separated and replanted in a fresh container and the process repeated if required. Each little plant is then transferred to a jelly containing a different combination of hormones that stops the process of rapid proliferation and causes the formation of roots instead. When they are sufficiently large the plantlets are weaned back into a conventional soil mixture and grown on in the usual way. Using this method it is possible to propagate many thousands of identical plants within a few months – a feat that is impossible to match by conventional means.

Although increased rate of propagation is one advantage of this method, it can also free plants from viral and bacterial diseases. These diseases circulate in the sap of plants and gradually invade new tissue as the plant grows. The newest cells at the growing tip of a plant are often disease free, and if removed under aseptic conditions can be grown on without their ever becoming contaminated. The process is also helped if the 'mother' plants are selected and tested for their freedom from disease, and are then given optimal conditions for rapid growth. Not every culture is successful in this respect, and further tests have to be performed to verify that the plants are clean. Sap-sucking insects such as aphids will quickly reinfect these plants, and to prevent this occurring the valuable virus-free stock (or indexed stock as it is sometimes called) is kept in sealed greenhouses supplied with filtered air under slight pressure. This nuclear stock is then used to propagate disease-free stock plants from which saleable stock is grown by conventional means.

Viruses often have a pronounced and debilitating effect on plant growth. However, the minor infections that occur in virtually all plants are often responsible for some of the accepted characteristics of that cultivar, and some of the older cultivars often take on a completely new appearance when they have been cleaned up by this method. Plants that were compact and bushy can become open and leafy and lose some of their charm. Many growers feel that, for certain cultivars, careful stock selection is better than freeing them completely from disease and destroying some of their established characteristics.

PROPAGATION FROM SEED

This method is becoming increasingly popular with commercial growers, and seed-raised strains of zonal pelargoniums have in many cases replaced those grown from cuttings. This is particularly true of many parks and recreation departments, which traditionally plant up large beds of these subjects. Some growers prefer double and semi-double cultivars, and these are still propagated vegetatively as reliable forms are not yet available from seed. Hybridists are working on this problem, and no doubt new double flowered strains will eventually be produced.

The past few years has seen the commercial launch of a type of cascading pelargonium (Breakaway series) and the first true seed-raised strain of an ivy leaf pelargonium ('Summer Showers'). Both these introductions produce single blooms and as yet do not match the best of the cutting-raised forms for earliness of flowering.

Modern regal pelargoniums do not produce much seed – certainly not enough to make them a commercial proposition. Many growers save the few seeds they can obtain and sow them themselves to produce new cultivars.

Most commercial seeds are F_1 (first generation) hybrids, and as these are rather expensive it is worth making an extra effort to ensure maximum germination. Always use fresh seed compost, preferably a soilless blend. For best results the temperature of the soil should be maintained at 21 to 24°C (70 to 75°F). The seeds are large enough to be handled individually, and they should be sown about 2.5 cm (1 in) apart, covered with a thin layer of compost and watered in using a watering can with a fine rose. Some seed houses supply scarified seed; these have had the seed coat thinned chemically or by abrasion as a means of improving the uniformity and rate of germination. The first seedlings can then appear in as little as 24 hours after sowing. They should be pricked out as soon as large enough to handle, either into trays or, better still, into small individual pots. All reliable seedsmen provide their own specific instructions and these should be followed carefully, but growers who save their own seed, or those who are producing new cultivars by hybridizing (see page 75) should follow the guidelines given above.

F_1 HYBRID SEED PRODUCTION

The majority of commercially available seed strains are F_1 hybrids. These are produced by crossing two inbred lines to obtain a new, uniform and vigorous cultivar.

It can be a rewarding experiment for growers to sow some seed saved from their own plants; a lot can be learnt from the process. Plants raised from the seed from a single specimen will often show remarkable variations in flower colour, height, vigour, etc. This can be very interesting to an amateur grower, though the plants would be of little value to a commercial grower who needs uniformly sized plants of a known colour and performance. A nurseryman also needs to be able to advise a customer at the time of purchase of the colour and ultimate height that a plant will attain.

If the seeds are sown from an attractive plant that has been deliberately fertilized with its own pollen there will still be a considerable lack of uniformity among the seedlings. Genetically the level of uniformity will improve at a rate of 50 per cent with every self-pollinated generation. If selection and self-pollination is carried out for a minimum of seven generations all variations will have been lost and the resulting seedlings will be identical. Although one goal has been realized, the process of inbreeding invariably decreases vigour and cultivars produced in this way have not been a great commercial success. However, if two of these inbred lines are crossed together the resulting seedlings should have hybrid vigour, and although they can be different in appearance from either parent they are uniform in all respects. These are the F_1 hybrids that are sold commercially. The final pollination for their production is made by hand, and to save the high cost of heating much of the seed production is carried out in India, Africa, Indonesia and Central America. The production of seed also acts as a filter for many plant diseases, and seedlings are generally free from the virus infections that can seriously debilitate many plants raised from cuttings.

'Deacon Lilac Mist' (see page 102) is the result of a cross between a miniature zonal and an ivy leaf pelargonium. The result has all the characteristics of the dwarf zonal pelargonium

A remarkable example of sporting within a single flower – 'Pink Bonanza' and 'Monkwood Bonanza' on 'Spot On Bonanza' (see page 77)

Because these hybrids are the first generation cross of two inbred lines, seed saved from them will not be uniform and the seedlings will show the separate characteristics of their two parents.

Recent advances in pollen grain culture (anther culture) may reduce the time taken to form the inbred strains for producing F_1 hybrid seed, and in the future this could decrease its cost.

Hybridizing

Hybridization is a process that uses the pollen from one plant to fertilize another. The usual aim is to combine the best features of both plants, but the results can be difficult to predict because of the genetic complexity of many hybrids. Raising plants from seed set by bees can be interesting, and has produced some exceptionally good cultivars. However, if the hybridist has a particular aim in mind, success will be more likely by following scientific methods.

The laws of heredity were first discovered by an Augustinian monk, Abbé Gregor Mendel, in the 19th century. A full discussion of these principles is beyond the scope of this book, but before embarking on serious hybridization it is helpful to understand the relevance of recessive characters. For example, the hybridist may wish to cross a beautiful white-flowered zonal pelargonium that has coarse, straggly growth with another that has bushy growth but a mediocre red flower, the idea being to produce a bushy plant with a beautiful white flower. The seedlings from this cross may all have red or pink flowers and the grower may appear to have failed. However, the chances are that the gene causing the white flower is recessive while the red is dominant, and that if two of

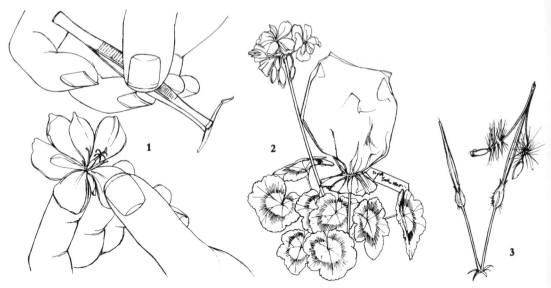

1. New hybrids can be produced by cross pollination which involves transfer of pollen from the stamen of one plant to the stigma of another;
2. Cover the pollinated flower with a paper bag and label;
3. Pelargonium seeds should be harvested as soon as they start to separate from the central style

the most bushy red or pink seedlings are cross-pollinated, white-flowered forms will occur in the next generation. A specific cross should never be judged by the appearance of the first generation seedlings but always carried on to the second generation, when the hoped for combination of characteristics may reappear.

The sexual organs of an individual pelargonium floret mature at different times, so it would appear that self-pollination is unlikely to occur. However, as florets on the same flowerhead will be at different stages of development, bees will transfer the pollen from other parts of the flowerhead and effect self-pollination in this way. If a planned series of crosses is to be made it is therefore essential that this process, and cross-pollination from other unwanted sources, should be prevented. The easiest method is either to place the mother plants inside a cage covered with fine netting or to cover each flowerhead individually with a muslin or paper bag. The bag must allow air and moisture to pass through it; plastic bags are quite unsuitable as developing seeds would quickly rot.

The actual process of cross-pollination is quite simple. The florets are inspected daily; as they mature the lobes of the stigma (see the diagram above) will be seen to unfurl. This is the stage at which they are receptive, and they will remain so for about 24 hours. A filament complete with a ripe anther should be pulled from the chosen male parent with a pair of tweezers, and the pollen dusted directly onto the stigma from the head of the anther. This should be repeated on the same flower using a different anther in case the pollen from the first one was not properly mature. If the stigma is examined with a lens the pollen grains should be seen adhering to it. The process should be repeated with any other flowers that seem to be at the receptive stage. Do not forget that to prevent unwanted self- or cross-pollination by bees it is essential to cover the flowers for a period several days before and after hand pollination has taken place. Tie a label giving the date of pollination and the name of the male parent to each flowerhead. Several double and semi-double flowers do not produce many anthers and pollen can be hard to find. In these circumstances a special plant should be grown to supply pollen by keeping it starved and confined to a small pot. Under these harsh conditions it will produce flowers with fewer petals and more pollen-bearing anthers. Even with this treatment it can be very difficult to obtain pollen from some of the ivy leaf pelargoniums. However, ripe pollen cannot always guarantee successful fertilization, as the parent plants may have different numbers of genes or other incompatibility factors.

If fertilization has occurred, within 10 days the characteristic long fruit will be seen growing from the centre of the flower. In the summer full ripening should occur in about six to eight weeks; the seed must be harvested as soon as the fruit splits, showing a white feathery tail. The seed should be removed from the outer covering before being sown as described earlier in this chapter.

If a good plant is obtained it should be considered for naming, but it is always advisable to seek a second opinion from another experienced pelargonium grower. A pelargonium nurseryman will often be willing to give advice and could also be interested in the new cultivar to add to his lists.

The plant should be named in accordance with the International Code of Nomenclature for Cultivated Plants, 1980. Since 1959 new names must not be in Latin; nor should a name be considered if it is already in use for another plant in the same genus. Names composed of numerals, abbreviations or a jumble of letters should be avoided, as should certain forms of address, e.g. Herr, Mademoiselle, Miss; but Madame, Mrs, etc. are allowed. It is also preferable to leave a cultivar name in another language unchanged. New cultivars should be registered with the appropriate International Registration Authority; in the case of *Pelargonium* and *Geranium* this is the Australian Geranium Society.

SPORTS

These are natural or artificially induced mutations that involve a genetic change in the plant. It produces a variation in a characteristic such as a change in flower colour or the production of variegated foliage. Sporting occurs quite frequently among pelargoniums, and some of the best cultivars have been produced in this way. The cause of this spontaneous mutation is not known but it is thought that its causes may involve the natural level of radioactivity, insect damage or exposure to various chemicals. These mutations can be artificially induced by radiation or by treatment of a young bud with colchicine, a very poisonous alkaloid extracted from species of *Colchicum*, the autumn crocus.

The sport occurs during the formation of the first few cells of a new shoot, and as it grows it exhibits the character of the new cultivar. When large enough, cuttings can be taken from this sport, and the resulting plants should retain the new characteristics. If a promising sport is noticed it should be allowed to grow to a reasonable size and then the energy of the plant diverted into it by pruning away the normal parts. At the same time a cutting or two of the sport can be taken and rooted. This should guarantee the establishment of the new cultivar.

Regal pelargoniums are particularly prone to sporting, and the sports themselves will occasionally revert back to the original parent or produce another new one. For example 'Pink Bonanza' has sported 'White Bonanza', 'Monkwood Bonanza', 'Spot on Bonanza' and a rose-pink cultivar as yet without a name. 'Grand Slam' has produced 'Lavender Grand Slam', 'Harewood Slam' and 'Lavender Harewood Slam'.

5
Pests and Diseases

In general, pelargoniums are robust and trouble-free plants, but there are a few pests and diseases that occasionally affect every collection. It is a wise precaution to examine all plants regularly, and if necessary to take remedial action without delay. If problems are caught early enough, it is usually relatively easy to control or eliminate them, whereas it is often a difficult or impossible task to cure an established outbreak. Weeds are a common cause of infection, particularly those growing by a greenhouse or under the staging inside it. No amount of hard work will eliminate a pest if reinfection can easily occur from a nearby source. However, do not be tempted to use weedkillers inside a greenhouse; many of them are volatile, and in a confined space plants can be seriously damaged by their vapour.

It is unfortunate that sooner or later regal pelargoniums will be attacked by whitefly, and zonal pelargoniums by rust disease, though this does not occur as commonly as a few years ago. Zonal pelargoniums can also suffer quite badly from virus infections, which are spread by aphids and other sap-sucking insects. Botrytis (grey mould) will attack all pelargoniums, particularly those growing in cold conditions where the air is still and moist. In normal circumstances, and apart from the problems mentioned above, all other pests and diseases are of relatively minor consequence.

Chemical sprays are a common and effective way of combatting pests and diseases. Unfortunately, after a period of use the chemical becomes much less effective or even totally inactive, because the pests produce resistant strains. Resistance to chemicals is often caused by improper application, and it is the responsibility of every user to ensure that they are applied carefully and in accordance with the manufacturer's instructions. For example, the insecticide resmethrin is now virtually inactive against whitefly; when it was first introduced the pests could be seen falling like snow within seconds of it being applied. The members of a colony of insects vary in their ability to withstand adverse conditions. If an insecticide is applied unevenly, or if the spray does not completely cover all parts of the plants, some of the insects will survive because they receive a sub-lethal dose. The survivors will obviously be the strongest in the colony, and have a higher than average resistance to the chemical in use. The next generation will have a statistically greater resistance to that particular chemical. This process will be repeated every time the insecticide is used, and as insects produce many generations a year resistant strains quickly appear. Permethrin, a more recently introduced analogue of resmethrin, has already become ineffective in many nurseries.

The insecticidal spray should be directed at all angles to ensure an even and thorough coverage of both the upper and lower sides of the leaves. Resistance cannot occur if a 100 per cent kill can be achieved; resistant strains will eventually appear as this goal can rarely, if ever, be obtained in practice. However, the effective life of the product will be prolonged. Do not be tempted to make up the

Opposite: Zonal pelargoniums are normally plants untroubled by pests or diseases

insecticide at a strength greater than that recommended, as it may damage the plants.

These comments apply mainly to 'contact insecticides', which require the active ingredient to come into direct contact with the insect. 'Systemic insecticides' are absorbed through the leaves and then distributed within the plant, and can kill sap-sucking insects that arrive many days or even weeks after the plant was first sprayed. As the concentration of the insecticide within the plant begins to weaken some of the pests will begin to survive, and resistant strains will then start to appear. The buildup of resistance should be slow, however, provided that the manufacturer's recommendations are observed regarding the interval between treatments. The same principles also apply to the formation of resistant strains of fungal diseases.

When an insect becomes resistant to a particular product it nearly always gains resistance to all other insecticides that are chemically related to it. For example, if a particular insect becomes resident to an organo-phosphorus insecticide, such as malathion, it will almost certainly be resistant to other closely related products, such as diazinon. To prevent a buildup of resistance it is a good idea to alternate the use of an insecticide or fungicide with a product containing a completely different active ingredient.

Chemical pesticides can be applied in a number of ways. The most common method of application is by wet spray, but they can also be applied as a smoke, a fog, from an aerosol can, or as an oil- or solvent-based formulation from an ultra low volume (ulv) sprayer. Because of their cost, fogging machines and ulv sprayers are normally used only by commercial growers.

Smoke cones, which look rather like fireworks, can be used to vaporize insecticides into the air, but not all of them are stable enough to be used in this manner. Smoke cones are an expensive way to buy chemicals and they obviously cannot be used out of doors, but in a greenhouse they are quick and convenient to use, and cover all parts of the plants including any overlooked weeds that may be growing under the staging.

Plants are likely to be damaged if treated in bright light or sunshine, so it is better to apply chemicals on a sunless day or, better still, in the evening after insects such as bees have departed for home.

The chemical names mentioned in this chapter are those of the active ingredients. Different manufacturers, though using the same active ingredients in their products, give them different names, and these can vary from country to country. The small print on the packaging should state the name or names of the active ingredients contained in each particular formulation. Sometimes a product will contain several active ingredients to give it a wider spectrum of activity. This sort of insecticidal or fungicidal 'cocktail' can be useful if the organism causing the trouble cannot be found or identified.

Some growers do not like using chemicals, and biological control of insect pests is gaining in popularity. This involves the introduction of either an insect or a fungus that preys on the pest without harming the plants or other beneficial insects such as bees. Under ideal conditions this method can work well, but it will fail if the temperature or humidity are not to the liking of the parasitic species. A different parasite is required to control each pest, and the combined use of biological and chemical control is not always possible. The parasites have to be reintroduced regularly as they tend to die out when the host starts to disappear. In addition to these drawbacks biological control can be very expensive. It is mainly used by commercial tomato and cucumber growers.

The names and addresses of biological control specialists can usually be obtained by sending a stamped addressed envelope to the advice column of a gardening magazine.

PESTS

Aphids (greenfly)
These small, usually wingless insects suck sap, and by moving from plant to plant spread incurable virus diseases. Large numbers of them severely weaken plants, and excrete a sticky substance that encourages the growth of unsightly sooty moulds. The insects can be green or bluish-green in colour, and at certain times of year they grow wings. As they grow the insects shed their old skins, the remains of which can be mistaken for whitefly.

Fortunately aphids are not particularly attracted to pelargoniums, but as they are very common insects they are frequently found in a collection of plants. Insecticides containing malathion, gamma HCH and diazinon are effective, and those containing dimethoate will kill the pests and also give continuous protection for up to three weeks. Derris, a natural plant extract, can also be used against them. Some enthusiasts grow marigolds in the greenhouse to attract hoverflies, whose larvae feed on greenfly.

Caterpillars
These are the larvae of moths; few butterflies will harm any of the pelargonium family. Outdoor zonal pelargoniums are often most affected, but plants growing in the greenhouse are sometimes attacked in the late summer and autumn. A few caterpillars can be removed by hand, but larger numbers are best controlled by spraying with an insecticide containing permethrin.

Sciarids
The adults are small black flies that are quite harmless; their larvae, however, can cause damage to young seedlings and cuttings. The flies, sometimes called fungus knats, are about 3 mm ($\frac{1}{10}$ in) long and lay their eggs in moist soil. They favour peat-based composts for this purpose, and have become much more common since soilless composts became popular. The larvae are wormlike, about 5 mm ($\frac{1}{5}$ in) in length, and virtually transparent. They live mainly on decomposing plant remains, but will attack young living tissue and the base of cuttings. It is not certain whether the larvae actually cause cuttings to rot or whether they move in and devour them after the rot has set in. It is probably better to be on the safe side and eliminate the pest before any damage is caused. Gamma HCH powder stirred into the surface of the soil is a good deterrent; drenching the soil with a solution of malathion will also eliminate the pest. Cuttings can be protected by dipping the ends into a mixture of 1 part by volume of gamma HCH powder mixed with 9 parts of hormone rooting powder. A similar quantity of powdered French chalk can be substituted for hormone rooting powder in the case of zonal and ivy leaf pelargoniums, which should not be treated with these preparations.

Spider mite (*Tetranychus urticae*)

This pest is widespread and can be a very serious problem, but it rarely causes severe damage to pelargoniums. The mites are tiny and virtually indiscernible to the naked eye. They spin a very fine web on the underside of the leaves, which eventually become brownish and speckled in colour and take on a dull and lustreless appearance. Red spider mite is now resistant to most organo-phosphorus insecticides such as malathion, diazinon and dimethoate, but azobenzene smokes still give a degree of protection. Pelargoniums should not be badly troubled by this pest, and it usually only attacks weak plants growing in a very dry atmosphere. Biological control is obtained by the introduction of the predatory mite *Phytoseiulus persimilis*.

Whitefly (*Trialeurodes vaporariorum*)

The adults have the appearance of small, white, wingless moths that fly away when disturbed. The juvenile stage is a small, flattened, scale-like creature, numbers of which can often be seen in groups attached to the undersides of leaves. They are commonly found on regal pelargoniums, and occasionally on zonal and ivy leaf pelargoniums. Like aphids, these insects excrete waste sugars obtained from plant sap, and black sooty moulds grow on these deposits.

Whitefly are now resistant to virtually all chemical pesticides, though aldicarb is often still effective. Unfortunately this substance is exceedingly poisonous, and its use is restricted to professional growers. Some retail nurseries also cannot use it because its toxic nature precludes public access for up to three weeks after use. Permethrin is a very safe insecticide, and although strains resistant to this chemical are now common it is still worth trying if it has not been used before. Currently whitefly are of great concern to all growers of fuchsias and regal pelargoniums, as these plants are among the most favoured hosts of this pest.

Adult whitefly have a very waxy coating that repels water, and to a certain extent this is responsible for their resistance to many insecticides. An amateur grower faced with a resistant strain of whitefly can try spraying them with a dilute solution of a detergent such as washing up liquid. This repels and weakens them by removing their protective layer of wax. The spray is made by adding a few drops of washing up liquid to about $\frac{1}{2}$ litre (1 pint) of water, and the solution applied to the plants in a fine but forceful spray, especially to the undersides of the leaves. If this treatment is not effective the concentration of detergent can be increased, but slight leaf damage might occur.

Recently small, sticky traps have been marketed that are claimed by the manufacturer to be attractive to whitefly. The traps are hung up between the plants like old-fashioned fly-papers. Time will tell whether this method will reduce whitefly numbers to a tolerable level.

Biological control is obtained by introduction of the parasitic wasp *Encarsia*. Black parasitized scales are bought from a specialist supplier; the adult wasps emerge from these, usually within a few days, and start to lay their eggs in new scales.

Other pests

Slugs, woodlice, mealy bug, thrips, cats and dogs can all cause damage to pelargoniums, but the trouble they cause is uncommon and often minor.

'Freak of Nature' (see page 104) has unusual variegation with white stems and leaves margined with green

DISEASES

Black leg

This disease mainly affects cuttings, but will sometimes attack mature plants. The first sign is usually a black mark at the base of the stem that rapidly spreads upwards, eventually causing the death of the plant. If the disease is at an early stage cuttings can be taken from the top of the stems, as they may not yet be infected.

Most authorities state that the fungus *Pythium* is responsible for this disease, but it is difficult to be certain whether this is the primary cause of the trouble or whether it only occurs as a secondary infection. It is a fact that pelargonium stems turn black when they die, from whatever cause. Gross overfeeding will produce the symptoms of black leg without any pathogenic fungus being present, so it is uncertain whether this disease really exists in its own right or is just a general manifestation of stem death. Provided that clean pots and compost are used this 'disease' should cause only occasional problems.

Black mould

This is not a disease but a harmless fungus that grows on the sugary excretions of sap-sucking insects such as aphids and whitefly. Once formed the mould is difficult to remove; in the summer, and after the cause has been eliminated, the plants can be placed out of doors to allow the action of rainfall gradually to clean away the unsightly deposits.

Botrytis (grey mould, *Botrytis cinerea*)

This aptly named disease is caused by a fungus, and the spores can be seen on affected parts as a furry grey coating. The spores germinate only in cool, damp and still conditions. An unventilated greenhouse in late autumn and early winter provides an ideal breeding ground, and at this time the disease is very common. It tends to disappear during cold weather as the action of the heating system dries the atmosphere. In the amateur's greenhouse this mostly applies to electrical heating apparatus, as many other systems expel moisture into the air (see also page 53).

Botrytis usually attacks only dead or dying material, so this should be picked off as a matter of routine. The plants can also be sprayed with a fungicide containing benomyl or iprodione, or fumigated with a smoke containing tecnazene. Unfortunately, resistant strains of this disease are common. Important factors in controlling the problem are good greenhouse hygiene and, whenever conditions allow, plenty of ventilation.

Galls

These are curious knobbly growths that appear at, or just below, soil level. They are quite common and are thought to be caused by a soilborne organism. The galls should be broken away from the main stem as soon as they are seen, or they will grow quite large and slow down the growth of the rest of the plant. This problem is especially common with miniature zonal pelargoniums, but it is not a serious disease and there is no evidence to show that it is transmitted via cuttings.

Pelargonium rust (*Puccinia pelargonii zonalis*)

As the scientific name implies, this is a disease of zonal pelargoniums. It used to be quite uncommon, even unknown in some countries, but it now occurs quite frequently. The upper side of the leaf shows a round yellow spot or spots, and on the corresponding part on the underside of the leaf raised circles of rusty brown material can be seen. These are the spores of the disease, which when ripe are like dust, and spread on the wind to contaminate other plants.

The main source of infection is by buying diseased plants from nurseries. This should not occur as professional growers have access to fungicides such as oxycarboxin, which are very effective in controlling the disease. Amateur growers should thoroughly examine all their plants, pick off any infected leaves and carefully place them in a plastic bag to avoid dispersing any of the spores. The plants should then be sprayed with a fungicide containing thiram, maneb or mancozeb. Spraying should be repeated at approximately 10-day intervals until the problem disappears.

Stem rot and wilt disease

Various stem rots and wilt diseases can be caused by bacterial or fungal infections. They are very difficult to diagnose properly, and even a plant pathologist needs laboratory facilities to be certain of the particular cause of many ailments. It is not worth trying to save plants that show symptoms of stem rot or yellow spotting of the leaves. These diseases are uncommon, and the best protection is to remove the affected plants and either burn them or wrap them in plastic sheeting and consign them to the rubbish bin.

Virus diseases

It is likely that all pelargoniums are infected with some viruses, but they do not greatly affect the growth of the plant. Sometimes the level of viruses within the plant increases, or they become infected with a particularly virulent strain, and then they do show definite signs of disease. Usually the leaves are crinkled and distorted and they can have yellow spots. The flowers often show streaks of green along with the normal colour. The symptoms are normally more prominent in winter, and may virtually disappear during the summer.

Virus diseases are transmitted by sap-sucking insects such as greenfly, and there is no known cure. All infected plants should be burned to prevent the spread of infection.

PHYSIOLOGICAL DISORDERS

Leaf discoloration

It is normal for a certain number of old leaves to turn yellow and die, and at this stage it is better to remove them in case they start to rot and spread infection to healthy parts of the plant. However, if abnormally large numbers of leaves suddenly turn yellow it is a sign that the plant has received some sort of check.

The symptoms of underwatering and of overwatering are the same. Overwatering causes the soil to become sour and eventually kills some of the plant roots. Without a proper root system the plant cannot take up enough water, so it begins to show the same signs as those caused by underwatering, i.e. it wilts and many of the lower leaves turn yellow and start to fall. It is up to the individual grower to decide which condition applies. Overall yellowness of the leaves can be caused by nutritional factors, nitrogen shortage being one of the most common.

When zonal pelargoniums are moved from the comfortable surroundings of a heated greenhouse to the open air the leaves often turn red. This reddening is only temporary, and the colouring disappears as the plants become acclimatized to the new conditions. A gradual 'hardening off' process will eliminate the sudden shock and lessen the likelihood of leaf discoloration. A sudden drop in temperature will also cause a temporary reddening of the leaves.

Oedema

This disorder usually affects ivy leaf pelargoniums, but to a minor degree it sometimes occurs on zonal pelargoniums. The undersides of the leaves become covered with raised, light brown, irregularly shaped areas. It is not a simple problem to understand as it can be caused by a number of factors. The visual symptoms are produced by the rupturing of plant cells on the underside of the leaves. This is usually attributed to a sudden increase in the sap pressure caused by watering a very dry plant. However, atmospheric humidity, which to some extent controls the transpiration of the plant, and nutrition, particularly the levels of calcium in the tissues, all play a part. The cure is to feed the plants, make sure that they do not become very dry in between waterings and, where possible, increase ventilation to improve their ability to transpire. Unsightly and damaged leaves will not recover, so the worst affected ones should be removed to improve the plant's appearance.

6
The Pelargonium Year

SPRING

This time of year is usually regarded as the start of the growing season, and watering can be increased as the days become warmer. Plants start to grow rapidly at this time, and any that were not pruned in the autumn should be attended to now. As soon as active growth is seen, it is worth repotting or potting-on every plant in the collection. While the plants are being handled is a good time to examine them for any signs of pests and diseases and to start making routine sprayings to counteract any problems that seem to occur regularly. Unless quickly checked, a pest or disease that starts to develop in the spring can reach epidemic proportions before the end of the year.

Cuttings can be taken from plants in a heated greenhouse in early spring. When well rooted, these plants can be put into hanging baskets, tubs, urns, etc. and kept growing in the greenhouse so that they can be placed out of doors in full flower when the weather becomes warmer.

Opposite: Blocks of pelargoniums make a brilliant contribution to this summer border

Left: Make sure the greenhouse is kept clean in autumn to keep a good show going for as long as possible

Exhibition plants should have the tips of the stems pinched to increase bushiness, and they should be turned round regularly to even out any irregularities in growth. Do not forget to leave an appropriate interval between the last pinch and the date of the show to allow sufficient time for flowers to develop. Take cuttings in the late spring to produce exhibition plants for the following season.

Open the ventilators on warm days to avoid spring sunshine raising the internal temperature of the greenhouse above 10°C (64°F). Pelargoniums do not like being forced, and they can suffer from physiological disorders by being kept in warm, moist conditions.

Apply shading to prevent an excessive temperature rise in hot weather and to protect cuttings from wilting.

SUMMER

Late spring and early summer is the start of the main flowering season for the majority of pelargoniums, but some will already have been flowering for many weeks. To ensure a continuous display the plants must be fed regularly or potted on into a larger container. Plants must not be allowed to become too dry at this time of year.

When danger of frost is past, plants that are well hardened off can be planted out of doors, and hanging baskets and urns that have been planted up under glass can also be placed in their summer positions.

Summer is the time when pests such as aphids and whitefly build up to large numbers, and unless checked will cause a great deal of damage. If a pest has become established spray or fumigate every four to five days until the outbreak is eliminated.

Cuttings can be taken and rooted without additional heat at any time during this period, but the best time is late spring to early summer and in late summer. Cuttings for large specimen plants for decoration or exhibition in the following season should be taken in early summer, and plants for restricted pot sizes are best taken in late summer or early autumn.

AUTUMN

Take cuttings now from any large plants that are going to be discarded before winter. Material for cuttings should be plentiful, and only the very best should be used or the quality of the plants may gradually decline.

Caterpillars can be troublesome at this time of year, and if they start to cause damage preventative sprays will be necessary; an occasional caterpillar will not do much harm. Botrytis will start to increase as soon as the days become cool and damp, so all leaves that are beginning to turn yellow should be removed before they start to decay. Keep the ventilators open as much as possible during the day and apply gentle heat on cold nights. Any plants from outside should be brought inside before they are damaged by frost. Prune back the plants quite hard at this time to reduce their size and open them up so that air can circulate freely between the stems.

Clean the greenhouse glass so that maximum light will be able to penetrate, and make any necessary repairs to the structure. The heating apparatus should be checked and overhauled if required. It is worth getting electrical wiring checked periodically to ensure that it is sound and that safety devices are all functioning properly.

Examine all the plants for any pests and diseases and take remedial action. Any surviving pests will overwinter and cause an early outbreak the following spring. Clean away any remaining debris or weeds from under the staging and leave no other hiding places where pests can hibernate.

Watering should be reduced to the minimum necessary to help keep a dry atmosphere. Discontinue feeding, or change to a fertilizer containing a higher percentage of potassium.

WINTER

Botrytis can be a problem at this time, so on bright days continue to ventilate the greenhouse as much as possible. When the weather becomes colder the problem will tend to disappear as (electric) heating will dry the atmosphere and prevent the botrytis spores from germinating. Water sparingly at this time of the year; plants will need watering only at infrequent intervals. Some pelargoniums will continue flowering through the winter period, and if the blooms tend to damp off before they are fully open they can be picked and taken indoors.

The minimum temperature maintained by the heating apparatus should be checked using a maximum–minimum recording thermometer. Plant losses will be high if the level recorded during the night is unacceptably low.

Send for catalogues from specialist nurserymen and place orders well in advance of the required delivery time. Remember that the most expensive plants in a nursery list may not necessarily be the best to buy. A high price may only indicate that it is new or is difficult to grow or propagate.

Gradually start to increase watering again as spring approaches, and open the ventilators whenever possible, even if only for an hour a day.

A to Z of Pelargoniums

Pelargoniums are the best plants of all to brighten up a city street
or seaside town

The following descriptions are not meant to be taken as a definitive listing of all the worthy species and cultivars. There are many other plants as good as those mentioned that have had to be omitted through lack of space. All the plants in this section are currently commercially available, but not every nursery will stock all of them, and their availability will vary from country to country. Many can be found in garden centres, but it is necessary to buy the less common ones from a specialist nursery. Their addresses are found in the classified advertisement pages of gardening magazines.

The name mentioned after each species is that of the person who first described it, names in parentheses refer to the person who changed the original name; names given after each cultivar are those of the raiser or the nursery that introduced it commercially. The date given is the earliest known listing in the literature or in a commercial catalogue.

SPECIES, HYBRIDS AND CULTIVARS WITH SCENTED FOLIAGE

P. crispum
(Bergius) L'Héritier 1774
The most commonly cultivated form of this species is the beautiful cultivar 'Variegatum'. The very bushy, short-jointed plant has small, crinkled green and yellow leaves that smell strongly of lemon oil. The flowers are small, pale mauve and rather insignificant. This cultivar needs a little extra warmth in winter, as it is susceptible to disease in cold, damp conditions.

P. echinatum
Curtis 1794
The flower colour of this species varies a great deal in the wild. *P. echinatum* 'Miss Stapleton' is available from specialist suppliers, but this may be only a purple-magenta-flowered form of the species. The white-flowered *P. echinatum* is also stocked by some nurseries. The rather small, primitive flowers are produced on a shrubby, succulent plant. The leaf stipules on this species are modified by becoming spine-like, presumably to act as a defence against grazing animals. It requires full light and careful watering, especially in the winter months.

P. filifolium
Knuth – date unknown
This species has attractive fern-like foliage that is slightly sticky to the touch. The scent is not strong and rather acrid in nature. The flowers are small and not very freely produced but the plant is well worth growing for its beautiful leaves.

P. fragrans
Willdenow 1800
This species has small, three-lobed leaves. The plant is much branched and compact. *P. fragrans* 'Variegata' (also listed as 'Snowy Nutmeg') has attractive white and green variegated leaves, and a slightly dwarfer habit than the green form. Both the species and the cultivar have a scent that is variously described as pine, nutmeg or lemon. All three odours can be detected; the one that predominates depends on individual opinion and how the plants are cultivated. When the old leaves have been covered by a canopy of new ones they soon turn yellow and die; to keep the plant looking tidy it is necessary to keep removing the dead and dying foliage. The small flowers are an off-white colour.

P. gibbosum
(Linnaeus) L'Héritier 1712
This is a shrubby, succulent plant whose stems are noticeably thickened at the nodes. The flowers are very small, but are an unusual deep greenish yellow. Interesting rather than beautiful.

P. graveolens
L'Héritier ex Aiton 1777
This is a strong, easy growing species. The leaves are roughly triangular and deeply five-lobed. The small flowers are pink, with purple spotting on the upper petals. The foliage has a strong smell of lemon; some authorities refer to it as an odour of orange.

P. inquinans
(Linnaeus) L'Héritier 1714
This species has primitive red flowers, and is thought to be the most important ancestor of *P. × hortorum*, the zonal pelargonium. It differs from *P. zonale*, another important ancestor of *P. × hortorum*, in a number of respects, one of the most noticeable being the lack of zoning on the leaf. Pink- and white-flowered forms have also been recorded.

P. × kewense
R. Dyer – Royal Botanic Gardens, Kew 1934
This is a primary hybrid and not a true species. It was found growing at Kew Gardens and is thought to be a hybrid between *P. inquinans* and *P. zonale*. The plant is dwarf and fairly free branching, and the narrow-petalled flowers are deep red. This plant has produced a sport with silver and white leaves called 'Silver Kewense'.

P. odoratissimum
(Linnaeus) L'Héritier 1724
This is a low-growing, rather spreading species. The mid green leaves are oval, almost rounded, and have a smell of apples. The rather insignificant white flowers are very freely produced.

P. peltatum
(Linnaeus) L'Héritier 1701
This species has five-lobed leaves with a small dark central zone, and a pronounced scrambling and pendant habit. This is the ancestor from which all the modern ivy leaf pelargoniums have been developed. The flowers are very variable in colour but are often white or lavender, spotted and veined with red.

P. scandens
Ehrhardt 1792
This is a large-growing, rather scrambling shrub. The leaves are strongly zoned and the flowers pink. The validity of this species is currently in doubt. The original description is not very informative and type specimens are not readily available. Some of the plants circulating under this name in Britain are in fact *P. frutetorum*, but

there is a possibility that hybrids are also being sold as this species.

P. tetragonum
(Linnaeus fil.) L'Héritier 1774
This is another very succulent species; the fleshy stems are normally four-angled and bright green in colour. The leaves are often sparsely produced, and are a dull green colour with a dark central blotch. The small flowers are a shade of rosy mauve.

P. tomentosum
Jacquin 1790
This is a large plant that requires frequent pinching or pruning to keep it to a manageable size and shape. The leaves are large, oval, and soft and velvety to the touch with a strong smell of peppermint. The flowers are white, freely produced but small and insignificant.

P. tricolor
Curtis 1792
This is a plant with a spreading habit. The leaves are a silvery greyish green. The very beautiful flowers have deep red upper petals and almost white lower petals with a darker blotch in the throat. Sometimes catalogued as *P. violareum*, but is is almost certainly a hybrid of *P. tricolor*. It is hoped to give this plant a clonal name in the near future.

P. zonale
(Linnaeus) L'Héritier c. 1700
The leaves of this species are crenate with only a faint zone, which is surprising considering its name. In the wild the flowers are variable in colour, and range from white to red or purple.

'Attar of Roses'
Cannell & Sons – Britain 1900
The plant has a fairly dwarf habit, and is bushy and self branching. The leaves have a scent of lemon, but there is a hint of rose in the background. The mauve flowers are small but freely produced. This hybrid imparts a beautiful and delicate flavour to cakes and sponges.

'Clorinda'
Cannell & Sons – Britain 1907
This hybrid will grow into a large plant, so

Pelargonium echinatum (see page 92)

occasional hard pruning is necessary to keep it bushy and at a manageable size. The pink flowers are quite large and attractive. The scent of the leaves has been variously described as cedar, eucalyptus or rose, but a cedar odour mixed with camphor is nearer the truth.

'Joy Lucille'
Origin unknown – before 1910
The name of this hybrid is sometimes spelt 'Joy Lucile'. The plant has an erect, vigorous habit and the leaves are deeply lobed in the manner of *P. graveolens*. The flowers are whitish and rather insignificant, and the leaves have a scent of peppermint.

'Lady Plymouth'
Origin unknown – c. 1880
The plant has a reasonably dwarf habit, and it will become bushy if the growing tips are pinched out. The deeply lobed, pale sage green leaves have a border of creamy white, and the small mauve flowers are freely produced. The odour of the leaves is variously described as rose or peppery citron, but there is also a note of camphor. A sport of *P. graveolens*, to which it sometimes reverts.

'Mabel Grey'
Origin unknown – Kenya 1960
The dark green leaves are rough and heavily serrated. They have an incredibly strong odour of lemon, the strongest scent of any of the *Pelargonium* species or

'Attar of Roses' (see page 93)

cultivars. The plant is rather slow-growing, and needs a minimum winter temperature of 10°C (50°F).

'Prince of Orange'
Origin unknown – before 1880
The smallish, rather rounded leaves are orange scented. The plant is thin stemmed and upright in growth, and needs frequent pinching to make it bushy. The medium sized flowers are pale mauve.

REGAL PELARGONIUMS

'Amethyst'
A. Pearce – Britain 1977
This cultivar received a First Class Certificate from the Royal Horticultural Society. The plant is extra compact and bushy, and the large, deep lavender-coloured flowers are produced in profusion. It makes an excellent pot plant.

'Aztec'
W. Schmidt – USA 1962
This cultivar once used to be the exhibitor's favourite, but it has been replaced on the show benches with newer introductions. It is still worth growing, as it is an excellent plant and exceptionally free flowering. The flowers are white, with a bold strawberry red marking on the centre of each petal.

'Beryl Reid'
J. Thorp – Britain 1975
The flowers are a deep salmon colour and

the petals are broadly marked with brownish black. This cultivar is very free flowering and compact, and has been successfully used by exhibitors.

'Break O'Day'
W. Schmidt – USA 1961
The flowers are white, faintly flushed dawn pink. This is not as free branching as some modern cultivars but is still acceptably compact and makes an attractive pot plant.

'Cezanne'
A. Janus – Britain 1962
A very beautiful regal, with deep royal purple upper petals and glistening white lower petals. Reasonably compact, and flowers slightly later than most others of this group.

'Dubonnet'
H. May – USA 1957
This cultivar is aptly named, for the flowers are a deep wine red. The centre of each petal is brownish red. Extra compact in growth, and very free flowering.

'Fringed Aztec'
Raiser unknown – USA c. 1977
This is a unique sport from 'Aztec'. The flowers are coloured white and strawberry red just like those of its parent, but the edges of the petals are heavily serrated, giving the plant a very unusual appearance. Slow growing, but bushy and floriferous.

'Grandma Fischer'
Raiser unknown – USA c. 1950
The flowers are a good deep orange colour, with a central blackish brown blotch on each petal. The foliage is a deep bluish green. There is reference to a 'Grandma Fischer' raised by Faiss before 1925, but its description does not match the one sold under this name today.

'Grand Slam'
W. Schmidt – USA 1950
Although it was raised in 1950, this is still the best red-flowered cultivar available. It received the Royal Horticultural Society's First Class Certificate in 1961. The flowers are a bright red with dark brownish red markings on the centre of each petal.

'Harewood Slam'
Origin and date unknown
This is a sport from 'Grand Slam', and has many of its parent's good qualities. The flowers are very variable in colour and are irregularly marked with deep brownish red and bright red. Very unusual.

'Hazel' see 'Purple Rogue'

'Hazel Cherry'
D. Fielding – Britain c. 1972
The compact and bushy plant bears cherry red flowers that are veined and blotched with deep red.

'Cezanne'

'Pompeii' (see page 97)

'Hazel Choice'
D. Fielding – Britain c. 1983
The flowers are a bright salmon-red with brownish orange veining. The plant is exceptionally free flowering and compact; very suitable for exhibition.

'Hazel Gypsy'
D. Fielding – Britain 1981
This is outstanding both as a decorative pot plant and as an exhibition cultivar. The petals are a luminous shade of light red, but have paler edges and a dark brownish red central marking.

'Hazel Herald'
D. Fielding – Britain c. 1972
This is a compact, almost dwarf cultivar, with unusual, deeply lobed leaves. White flowers, marked with blood-red.

'Hazel Perfection'
D. Fielding – Britain 1981
This cultivar can be disappointing as a small plant, as the stems are rather thin and wiry. When grown to a reasonable size, or grown on for a second season, it excels as a decorative or show specimen. The medium sized flowers are deep purple in colour and are produced in profusion. It also has a naturally neat shape and grows in the form of a flattened dome. Highly recommended.

'Inca'
East Lynne Gardens – Britain c. 1975
This is a dwarf, rather slow growing plant. The stems are thin and at first look unpromising, but its true potential is realized as it matures. Growth is exceptionally bushy. The upper petals are deep red and the lower petals pale pink. Because of their compact and dwarf nature, this and similar cultivars, such as 'Vicky Town', are well suited to growing in the house as windowsill pot plants.

'Jennifer Strange'
D. Clark – Britain 1985
The extra large flowers are a deep, glowing orange-red, with a pronounced white throat and white edges to each petal. The plant will grow large but is reasonably bushy and self branching.

'Joan Morf'
G. Morf – Australia date unknown
The flowers are pale pink, with a pronounced white throat and broad white petal edges. The blooms are ruffled and very appealing. The growth is bushy and the leaves are light green.

'Lavender Grand Slam'
W. Schmidt – USA 1953
This is a sport from 'Grand Slam'; the mutual reversion/mutation between the two cultivars is quite common. The flowers are a bright shade of lavender, and it has all its progenitor's fine qualities.

'Lavender Harewood Slam'
Origin and date unknown
This is a sport either from 'Harewood Slam' or from 'Lavender Grand Slam'. In theory both these plants could mutate to produce it. The flowers are a dark, velvety red, irregularly streaked with bright lavender. Very spectacular and eye-catching.

'Marie Rober'
E. Rober – USA 1937
The flowers are ruffled and an outstanding deep royal purple colour. The plant growth is fairly vigorous, and it tends to grow taller than it is broad.

'Market Day'
A. Pearce – Britain 1977
The flowers are a pale shade of lavender-pink. They are produced in great profusion on an extra compact, bushy plant. Suitable as a pot plant or for exhibition.

'Marquita'
W. Schmidt – USA 1966
The flowers are extra large, and a beautiful shade of salmon-orange. This plant is exceptionally free flowering, and although its growth is not as compact as many other cultivars it makes an excellent exhibition plant.

'May Magic'
H. May – USA 1965
The slightly ruffled flowers are a pale salmon-orange, with a paler throat and petal edges. A pleasing colour combination with reasonably bushy and compact growth.

'Monkwood Bonanza'
D. Clark – Britain 1985
This is a sport from 'Pink Bonanza' and differs from its parent in having paler, clear pink flowers. Like its parent, this cultivar is very compact and bushy and flowers profusely over a long period.

'Monkwood Charm'
D. Clark – Britain 1980
The large flowers have a deep red central mark on each petal, surrounded by a wide border of salmon-orange. The plant is compact and free flowering. An 'Aztec' seedling.

'Monkwood Delight'
D. Clark – Britain 1980
The bright lavender petals have a large central marking of deep purple. The large flowers are produced freely on compact growth. An 'Aztec' seedling and a sister of 'Monkwood Charm'. Similarly marked flowers are produced by 'Hazel Satin', but the ground colour is paler.

'Monkwood Dream'
D. Clark – Britain 1983
The extra large flowers are a bright pink with a silvery pink reverse. The plant is naturally compact and bushy, and starts to flower very early in the season.

'Monkwood Rhapsody'
D. Clark – Britain 1985
The upper petals are orchid purple with orchid pink edges. The lower petals have a well-defined band of pale orchid purple, with white edges and a white throat. Originated as a seedling from 'Sunrise'.

'Morwenna'
H. Parrett – Britain c. 1964
A pure, deep purplish black flower. Compact, with very bushy growth, this is probably the best of the 'black' regals. Other good dark cultivars include 'Dark Venus', 'Fifth Avenue' and 'Minstrel Boy'.

'Mrs G. Morf'
G. Morf – Australia date unknown
The flowers are ruffled and an unusual shade of purplish plum. The growth is very bushy; this cultivar makes an excellent show plant.

'Nimrod'
A. Pearce – Britain 1987
The upper petals are maroon with white edges; the lower petals are white with slight red veining. A new cultivar that shows great promise.

'Phyllis Brooks'
D. Clark – Britain 1986
The flower is a bright orange with a pronounced white throat and white edges to the petals. It is compact and bushy – a very attractive regal.

'Pink Bonanza'
W. Schmidt – USA 1966
The flowers are a bright pale salmon-orange colour; almost a self. The growth is compact and bushy; the plant starts to flower very early in the year and continues throughout the summer and often into early winter. This is the parent of a number of interesting and valuable sports. Along with 'Grand Slam' it must rate as one of the best two regals yet produced – and they were both raised by William E. Schmidt of Palo Alto, USA.

'Pompeii'
W. Schmidt – USA 1964
The flowers are a deep brownish black, with a narrow border of white around the petal edges. A similarly marked cultivar is 'South American Bronze', but the ground colour is paler and the flowers are noticeably smaller.

'Purple Rogue'
Origin and date unknown
This is a purple sport from 'Rogue'; the same sport has been named 'Purple Gown' and subsequently 'Hazel'. It is now mostly catalogued under the latter name, but according to the International Laws of Nomenclature the name in more current use should be used. This is still one of the best purple regals in cultivation.

'Rembrandt'
G. Morf – Australia c. 1972
This is a large cultivar, but it is still reasonably bushy and self branching. The centre of each petal is deep purple surrounded by a lighter shade of the same

'Lavender Harewood Slam'

colour. The edges of the petals have a distinct border of pale lavender.

'Rogue'
W. Schmidt – USA 1955
The flowers are deep red, each petal having a dusky central marking. The plant is exceptionally bushy and self branching, and is often used as a small decorative pot plant.

'Rosmaroy'
R. Hollihead – Britain c. 1982
This free flowering cultivar produces a mass of medium sized, frilled flowers on a compact, bushy plant. The flower colour is an unusual shade of lavender-pink; some nurseries describe it as having a bluish tinge. One of the best of the recent introductions.

'Spot On Bonanza'
D. Fielding – Britain 1985
This is another remarkable sport from 'Pink Bonanza'. The white flowers are irregularly speckled and streaked with salmon pink. 'Spot On Bonanza' is the first regal pelargonium to show this type of coloration, and it has all the virtues of its famous parent. Undoubtedly a new and dramatic breakthrough.

'Sunrise'
'Spot On Bonanza' (see page 96)

W. Schmidt – USA 1967
The large flowers are a light shade of

orange, but the throat and petal edges are white. The flower colour can change quite dramatically depending on the balance between nitrogen and potassium in the compost. When the plant has recently been repotted, or if it is fed with a high nitrogen fertilizer, the flower colour becomes almost pink; if it is fed with a high potassium feed the colour changes to a beautiful coppery orange.

'Vicky Town'
A. Pearce – Britain 1972
This is a slow growing, almost dwarf cultivar, but it produces a tremendous show of flowers. The habit is extra compact and bushy. The flowers are a purplish plum, shading to deep mauve towards the petal edges. Because of its small size it makes a good house plant.

'Wellington'
Origin and date unknown
This cultivar has deep orange flowers with central markings of a deep coppery brown. The habit is bushy and self branching, and it is exceptionally free flowering. A similarly coloured cultivar is 'Dunkery Beacon'.

'White Bonanza'
F. Biddlecombe/Thorps Nurseries and D. Clark – Britain 1984
This sport from 'Pink Bonanza' is virtually pure white, with only tiny purple pencil marks appearing on the upper petals. The plant is very bushy and starts to flower

early in the season. The sport appeared in at least two collections in the same year. Other good white-flowered regal pelargoniums include 'Mercia Glory', 'Grandma Ross' and 'White Chiffon'.

ANGEL PELARGONIUMS

'Catford Belle'
A. Langley Smith – Britain 1935
This is a compact plant that bears masses of mauve-purple flowers, the upper petals of which are marked with a deeper shade of purple.

'Madame Layal'
Raiser unknown – France c. 1870
The upper petals are a deep plum-purple colour with white edges; the lower petals are white with purple central markings. One of the most attractive members of the group.

'Mrs H. G. Smith'
A. Langley Smith – Britain 1940
The upper petals are a pinkish mauve shade with a white edge; the lower petals are white. This is a compact, bushy cultivar

and it has the added advantage of lemon-scented leaves.

'Rita Scheen'
Gerris – Britain 1978
This is the first recorded angel pelargonium with variegated foliage. The flowers are a soft lilac colour, with a maroon blotch and feathering on the upper petals.

'Sancho Panza'
Telston Nurseries – Britain date unknown
The flowers are a pure shade of deep purple with lavender-purple edges to the petals. A very attractive cultivar.

UNIQUE PELARGONIUMS

'Claret Rock Unique'
Origin and date unknown
This is sometimes referred to simply as 'Claret Rock'. The flowers are a pale claret colour, and the two upper petals have bold markings of brownish red. Like all the plants in this group, it is a vigorous, upright grower, with stems that soon become woody.

'Madame Layal'

'Madame Nonin'

Nonin — country unknown 1870

This is one of the best-known members of the group. The habit is free branching, and more compact than usual. The very attractive tyrian rose-coloured flowers are frilled and overlaid with red. The leaves have an attractive scent.

'Rollison's Unique'

Rollison — country unknown, before 1880

This is a good, reasonably compact cultivar with magenta-red flowers. The upper petals have broad markings of purple. The leaves are pleasantly rose scented.

'Voodoo'

F. Hartsook — Mexico 1972

A tall-growing cultivar, this has very attractive, deep velvety red flowers with black markings on the centre of the petals, and triangularly shaped leaves. A very striking cultivar.

ZONAL PELARGONIUMS

'A Happy Thought'

Lynes — Britain 1877

This handsome cultivar is easily recognized by the marking on its leaves. The centre is pale yellow or greenish yellow, surrounded by a diffuse brown zone and a broad, bright green leaf edge. The flowerheads are composed of small, single red florets.

'Alex'

W. Elsner — E. Germany date unknown

The semi-double flowers are a striking shade of brilliant scarlet. It is very free flowering, and exceptionally easy to grow and propagate. The leaves are deep green and slightly velvety; the plant is compact and well branched. Excellent for bedding.

'Alcyone'

Raiser unknown — USA 1968

This is a miniature with dark, blackish green foliage and deep crimson double flowers. An easy plant to grow. One source has listed 'Alcyone' as having single pink flowers, so there may be more than one cultivar sharing this name.

'Apple Blossom Rosebud'

Raiser unknown — USA date unknown

This is a typical member of the Rosebud or Noisette group of zonal pelargoniums. The double flowers are tightly packed, so each individual floret looks like a partially open rosebud. The flowers are pale pink flushed with deeper pink, and all the colours deepen noticeably with age. The growth is upright, and it needs to be pinched early to encourage a bushy shape.

'Arctic Star'

E. Both — Australia, before 1963

This cultivar shows the typical characteristics of the stellar group in having deeply lobed leaves and curiously forked petals; the flower is an icy white. The habit is moderately compact and bushy.

'Ashfield Monarch'

G. Massheder — Britain 1975

This cultivar is similar in many respects to 'Alex', but the flower colour is less vivid and a more crimson shade of red. It propagates easily, and the semi-double flowers have good weather resistance.

'Beacon Hill'

I. Gillam — Canada, before 1985

This is a single-flowered miniature with dark green foliage. The flowers are a shade of carmine with a large white centre.

'Beryl Gibbons'

J. Gibbons — Britain 1981

This is an excellent white double-flowered cultivar. The plant is short jointed and free branching and is similar to 'Regina', which is one of its parents. It makes an excellent show plant.

'Bird Dancer'

M. Bird — USA date unknown

This is a dwarf plant, with dark-zoned leaves of the stellar group. The pale salmon blooms are thin and spidery.

'Blues'

Fischer — W. Germany date unknown

An excellent bedding cultivar that has pink, semi-double flowers with a white centre. Growth is vigorous but compact and bushy.

'Bold Appleblossom'

J. Gibbons – Britain 1985

The large single flowers are an apple blossom pink colour, pale at the petal edges but deepening towards the centre. The flowerheads are sturdy and well formed. This is an excellent cultivar, which unlike many other singles does not easily shed petals while being transported.

'Bold Sunrise'

J. Gibbons – Britain 1986

This is a new cultivar so it still has to stand the test of time. However, the deep salmon, semi-double flowers and strong but bushy growth should ensure that it has a great future.

'Bold Sunset'

J. Gibbons – Britain 1985

The double flowers are a pale salmon-orange colour, deepening noticeably in the centre. The habit of growth is short jointed and bushy.

'Brenda Kitson'

K. Kitson – Britain 1982

The double flowers are a pale rose-pink with a white centre. The plant is excepionally stocky and short jointed.

'Burgenlandmadel'

Polatschek Bros – Austria 1964

This is an excellent cultivar with deep pink, very double flowers. The habit is stocky and short jointed and the leaves are attractively zoned. A good cultivar for exhibition and indoor use, but unfortunately in wet weather the flowerheads damp off very readily. Also known as 'Burgenland Girl'.

'Carole Monroe' ('Carol Monroe')

K. Gamble – Britain 1971

This is an exceptionally compact plant. The enormous lavender-pink flowerheads are produced in profusion. The florets are very tightly bunched together, which leads to damping off problems in unfavourable weather conditions.

'Caroline Schmidt'

Raiser unknown – Germany before 1900

This is an excellent old cultivar that has not yet been surpassed. The rather crinkled leaves are silvery green with a creamy white edge. The florets are double and an intense bright red colour, but the flower-heads themselves are not large. The growth is upright and the stems need pinching to obtain a bushy plant. Very suitable as a bedding plant, either for massed effect or as a dot plant among other green-leaved pelargoniums.

'Chattisham'

R. Bidwell – Britain 1978

'Chattisham' is a miniature with greenish gold, rounded leaves with a brownish zone. The rather small single flowers are white, but turn pink with age and have distinct vertical red pencilling on all petals.

'Cheiko'

H. Parrett – Britain 1968

The large double flowers are in shades of crimson and purple. This is a dense-growing miniature with medium to large mid green leaves.

'Chelsea Gem'

Bull – country unknown 1880

Like 'Caroline Schmidt', this cultivar has silvery green leaves with a cream edge. The double flowers are pale pink with a whitish centre. The flowerheads are not large but they are freely produced. The growth is bushy; it will make a good pot plant and is also very useful for bedding. A similar if not identical cultivar is 'Mrs Parker'.

'Contrast'

Merry Gardens – USA before 1970

The tricoloured leaves are similar in appearance to those of 'Mrs H. Cox', but if anything more brilliantly coloured. The centre of the leaf is light green and is surrounded by blackish red and bright red. The edges of the leaves are yellow with splashes of green. Flowers are single, red, and rather insignificant. This is even slower in growth than 'Mrs H. Cox', but with care it can be a very rewarding plant.

'Countess Mariza'

Polatschek Bros – Austria before 1968

This is a short-jointed cultivar with leaves

that are velvety to the touch. The beautiful semi-double flowers are an unusual shade of deep pink. Good for bedding purposes. Also known as 'Gräfin Mariza'.

'Deacon Bonanza'
S. Stringer – Britain 1970
The habit of this plant is typical of many of the Deacon group. The plant is very bushy and self branching. The deep lavender-pink, double flowers are produced very freely, but there are fewer than normal florets to each head.

'Deacon Fireball'
S. Stringer – Britain 1970
'Deacon Fireball' is a low-growing cultivar that can outgrow dwarf status; less free branching than others in its group. The double florets are an intense scarlet.

'Deacon Lilac Mist'
S. Stringer – Britain 1970
This is arguably the best of the Deacon group; it is certainly one of the most popular dwarf cultivars. The rounded, pale green leaves are formed on a compact,

very free branching plant, and the double flowers are produced in profusion. The blooms open a pale lavender-pink that deepens considerably with age, giving the flowerheads a bicoloured appearance.

'Deacon Minuet'
S. Stringer – Britain 1973
The habit of this dwarf cultivar is similar to that of 'Deacon Lilac Mist', but it has a more pronounced zone on the leaves. The double flowers are in two shades of soft peachy pink.

'Deacon Peacock'
S. Stringer – Britain 1977
An interesting dwarf plant with variegated leaves; it tends to grow taller and is less free branching than usual for a Deacon, but it is still well worth growing. The centre of the leaf is a pale greenish yellow, surrounded by a zone of a dark chocolate colour with flecks of chestnut brown. The leaf edges are dark green. The double flowers, larger than usual, are a nice deep orange with a silvery orange reverse.

'Contrast' (see page 101)

'Deacon Suntan'

S. Stringer – Britain 1979
The pale green leaves have an indistinct, rather diffuse zone, and the double flowers are a glorious shade of pale orange. Dwarf, but not as free branching as others in this group.

'Denebola'

S. Stringer – Britain 1967
The pale mauve-pink, semi-double flowers have a pale, almost white centre; the leaves are deep green. This miniature is of good constitution and easy to grow.

'Distinction'

Henderson – country unknown 1880
This is an unusual cultivar with deep green leaves and a narrow black zone near the serrated leaf edges. The stems are rather thin, and the plant is naturally bushy, low and spreading in habit. The small, red, single flowers are not produced very freely, but this does not matter as the plant is worth growing for the appearance of the leaves alone. Also known as 'One-in-a Ring'.

'Dolly Vardon'

Morris – country unknown 1880
The leaves of this cultivar are a rather dull greyish green surrounded by brownish red with a few streaks of bright red and edged with pale yellow. Although the colours are not as bright as 'Mrs H. Cox' or 'Contrast', this cultivar grows in a more bushy fashion

and is much easier to grow during the winter. The flowers are small, single and vermilion red in colour.

'Dovedale'

A. Shellard – Britain 1983
This is a very nice plant, with golden yellow leaves, but like the leaves of all members of the group they can turn rather greenish if overfed. It is thought to be the first pelargonium with nearly double white flowers and gold-coloured leaves. The plant is very bushy and low growing, almost dwarf. Although the white flowers do not show up very well against the yellow foliage, this cultivar is well worth growing.

'Dwarf Miriam Baisey'

F. Read – Britain 1950
This plant is also catalogued as 'Dwarf Miriam Baisy' and 'Dwarf Miriam Bassy'. It has single, bright red flowers with a white centre. The relative amount of each colour is quite variable, and the size of the central white patch alters considerably. Very free flowering.

'Emma Hossler'

H. Miller – USA date unknown
This cultivar perfectly mimics in dwarf form the typical habit of many full-sized zonal pelargoniums. The leaves do not have a noticeable zone and are a pale green colour. The double flowers are a shade of soft pink.

'Deacon Peacock'

'Gemini' (see page 104)

'Falklands Hero'
A. Shellard – Britain 1983
This relatively new member of the tri-colour leaf group has more muted colours than either 'Contrast' or 'Mrs H. Cox', but the habit is much more short jointed and bushy. The leaves are green in the centre and yellow at the edges, with a red zone over the junction of these two colours. It is suitable for use as a bedding plant, when the colour of the leaves will become more intense. The smallish flowerheads are composed of single red florets.

'Fenton Farm'
T. Portas – Britain 1981
This is a compact plant with deep golden yellow leaves without noticeable zoning. The flowers are single, a vivid purple with a white centre, and contrast sharply with the colour of the leaves.

'Fleurette'
Case – Britain 1955
An excellent miniature for the beginner as it grows and propagates easily. The large double flowers are a salmon-pink colour. Deep green leaves.

'Frank Headley'
F. Headley – Britain 1957
'Frank Headley' is a dwarf that is un-doubtedly one of the most free flowering zonal pelargoniums yet produced. The salmon-pink single florets are primitive in form but are produced in such profusion that they completely hide the silvery green, white-edged leaves. With maturity or generous treatment it can easily out-grow the dwarf classification. This cultivar needs protection from the elements and flowers more freely in the greenhouse than it does in the open.

'Freak of Nature'
Gray – country unknown 1880
This cultivar is well named, as it reverses the normal pattern of colouring in pel-argoniums. The main stems, leaf petioles and flower stalks are white, and the wavy leaves are white with a narrow green edge. The plant is reasonably short jointed and bushy. The single red flowers look attract-ive against the light-coloured foliage.

'Friary Wood'
S. Peat – Britain before 1970
The large, well-formed double flowers are a deep shade of pinkish mauve. The leaves are gold with a pronounced chestnut zone. Growth is short jointed, compact and bushy.

'Frills'
H. Miller – USA date unknown
An unusual miniature with salmon-pink double flowers. The petals are long and narrow and are rather ragged in appear-ance. The medium-small leaves are deep green, slightly cupped and distinctly lobed. Said to be a cross between *P. acetosum* and the miniature zonal pelar-gonium 'Minx'.

'Gemini'
Fischer – West Germany 1982
This is one of the stellar group and has bright red flowers with white centres. The typical deeply lobed leaves have a just discernible dark zone. A striking cultivar that always seems to command attention.

'Geoff May'
H. Parrett – Britain date unknown
This miniature produces large single flowers in a shade of porcelain rose with a pronounced white centre. The leaves are deep green with a good dark zone.

'Goblin'
Kerrigan – USA 1955
This is a miniature that produces brilliant red, ball-shaped heads of double flowers. The leaves are a blackish green colour. It seldom exceeds 13 cm (5 in) in height, but still grows well and is fairly easy to propagate.

'Golden Crest'
H. Parrett – Britain before 1960
The leaves of this cultivar are a clear, unmarked golden yellow, but they tend to go greenish if the plant has recently been repotted or is being overfed. The smallish single flowers are a salmon-orange colour. This plant performs very well out of doors, and can be found for sale in some enterprising garden centres.

'Golden Ears'
I. Gillam – Canada c. 1982
'Golden Ears' is regarded as the first of the stellar group with bronze foliage. The growth is dwarf and the leaves have a green edge. The flowers are an orange-red colour. Similar cultivars, also raised by Ian Gillam, are 'Mrs Pat', with salmon-pink flowers, and 'Vancouver Centennial', with red flowers.

'Golden Harry Hieover'
Cannell & Sons – Britain 1880
The leaves are a pale green that changes to a golden green if the plant is slightly starved. The pronounced zone is a deep chestnut brown. The single, rather primitive flowers are bright scarlet and produced in profusion.

'Golden Staph'
E. Both – Australia date unknown
This is the first of the stellar group with a gold leaf and bronze zone. The plant is medium sized and grows larger than 'Golden Ears'. The salmon-orange flowers are freely produced.

'Highfield's Attracta'
K. Gamble – Britain 1971
The plant is bushy, short jointed and self branching, and is typical of the growth of many Highfield's cultivars raised from 'Regina'. The large double flowers are white, with salmon-pink in the centre and at the edge.

'Highfield's Choice'
K. Gamble – Britain 1977
The leaves of this excellent cultivar are dark green with a well-marked zone, and the plant is compact, bushy and self branching. The large, single, lavender-pink florets form medium sized, ball-shaped flowerheads. 'Ashfield Serenade' is similar in some respects but has single, lavender-coloured flowers, and leaves that lack zoning; it also has the bad habit of producing short flower stems that do not properly clear the foliage.

'Highfield's Festival'
K. Gamble – Britain 1974
The semi-double florets form medium sized flowerheads, and the habit of the plant is compact, bushy and self branching. Flower colour is a pale lavender-pink with a white centre. A good all-round bedding cultivar, but it does not propagate freely enough to be popular with large-scale commercial growers.

'Highfield's Pride'
K. Gamble – Britain 1972
This is a magnificent cultivar with single flowers. The deep crimson blooms are large and perfectly formed, and the leaves are dark green with a well-marked black zone. The plant habit is bushy and short jointed. 'Highfield's Pride' is very free flowering and makes an excellent bedding plant.

'Highfield's Sugar Candy'
K. Gamble – Britain 1971
The plant habit is compact and is typical of many other Highfield's cultivars. The double flowers are pale pink, almost white, but deepen with age, giving the blooms a bicoloured appearance.

'Hunters Moon'
T. Portas – Britain 1979
The single flowers are a magnificent deep glowing orange colour that contrasts beautifully with the golden leaves. The plant growth is compact and bushy, and it is surprising that this cultivar is not more widely grown.

'Irene'
C. Behringer – USA c. 1942
This was the first of a new collection of hybrids, and gave its name to the whole group. The Irenes are characterized by their strong but bushy, free branching growth, and their free flowering ability. After a while almost any plant that vaguely fitted these criteria was called an Irene even though they were genetically unrelated. Most of the group have semi-double flowers, which are borne in large trusses. All the Irenes are good for bedding but are now being replaced by newer cultivars. 'Irene' itself has bright cerise-red flowers, and was named after the wife of the raiser.

'Jane Eyre'

'Jane Eyre'
S. Stringer – Britain 1970
'Jane Eyre' is one of the most popular miniatures yet raised. It has large double flowerheads of lavender-pink; the leaves are dark green and well zoned.

'Kathleen Gamble'
K. Gamble – Britain 1966
Although double-flowered cultivars always seem to be more popular than singles, this one is always in demand. The growth is adequately bushy and self branching, and the flowers are a deep salmon colour, darker in the centre of the flower and lightening to pale pink at the petal edges. The flower colour can vary quite markedly, especially between winter and summer. The leaves are dark green and are broadly zoned in black.

'Keepsake'
H. Miller – USA 1962
'Keepsake' is a borderline plant between a miniature and a dwarf. The large double flowers are a strong rose-purple colour with some white in the centre. The leaves are dark green with slight zoning.

'Lady Ilchester'
Cole – Britain 1915
This old cultivar tends to grow rather tall; to produce a bushy plant it is necessary to pinch the growing tips out when the plant is small. The leaves are a pale soft green and the double flowers are a beautiful lavender colour.

'Lass O'Gowrie'
P. Grieve – Britain 1860
This is a slow-growing plant, and with care can be kept as a dwarf. The leaves are greyish green, with a cerise zone and a wide cream-coloured edge. The small single flowers are red and are not an important feature.

'Maréchal MacMahon'
Laing – Britain? c. 1872
This is a compact, bushy plant that produces a dense covering of leaves. The foliage is yellow (or tends to green if well fed) with a broad mahogany-brown zone. The small, red, single flowers are relatively insignificant. Similar in appearance is 'Patchwork Quilt', but this has deep salmon-coloured flowers.

'Marmalade'
F. Hartsook – USA or Mexico 1968
A miniature cultivar with double soft orange flowers that are held well clear of the blackish green foliage. Very free flowering. The raiser, Miss Hartsook, was an American who lived in Mexico.

'Mars'
Fischer – W. Germany c. 1985
The flowers of this superb bedding plant are a very bright scarlet, almost identical to that of 'Alex'. The habit of growth is short and bushy; the leaves are only faintly zoned. The semi-double flowers have very good weather resistance.

'Hunter's Moon'
(see page 105)

'Miss Burdett-Coutts'

P. Grieve – Britain 1869

This is another slow-growing plant, which superficially resembles 'Lass O'Gowrie'. The leaves have a green central marking, surrounded by a red zone with a wide border of creamy white. The rather uninteresting red single flowers are best removed, as they are formed on weak stems and tend to spoil the appearance of the plant.

'Miss Wackles'

S. Stringer – Britain 1970

The double flowers are large and a rather unusual shade of purplish red, and are held well clear of the sturdy, dark green leaves.

'Modesty'

F. Bode – USA 1965

This is said to be a seedling from 'Irene', and it certainly has the characteristics of this group. The white double flowers are nearly always tinged with pink. A nice cultivar, but many stocks seem to be troubled by virus disease and there are now better white-flowering cultivars available, such as 'Carol Gibbons'.

'Morval'

T. Portas – Britain 1976

An excellent dwarf that in overall appearance resembles some members of the Deacon group. The leaves are golden yellow with a light chestnut-brown zone. The leaves go greenish very easily if slightly overfed. The pale pink double flowers are produced in profusion.

'Mr Wren'

Conn/Wren – USA date unknown

The single flowers are a light red colour, with a white or pinkish edge often striped or spotted with red. The flowerheads are not large but they are attractive and unusual. The plant growth has long inter-

'Marmalade'

nodes, and is unfortunately tall and un-branching. It needs early and frequent pinching to encourage bushiness.

'Mrs H. Cox'
Cannell & Sons/Turner – Britain 1879
This old cultivar is also listed as 'Mrs Henry Cox', 'Mr Henry Cox' or just 'Henry Cox'. There seem to be a number of different clones of this plant in cultiv-ation, some of them more brightly col-oured than others. Good forms of it are similar to 'Contrast', but poorer ones are duller in appearance and therefore inferior. The leaves are irregularly marked, with shades of green surrounded by brownish red and bright red with a yellow border. The flowers are single and salmon-pink in colour. Frequent and early pinching is required to form a bushy shape, as the plant does not branch freely. This plant grows slowly, but faster than 'Contrast'.

'Mrs Pollock'
P. Grieve – Britain 1858
This beautiful cultivar has a mid green central patch with a heavy chocolate-brown zone splashed with bright red. The deeply lobed leaf margins are yellow. The smallish single flowers are an orangey red colour. The plant is much easier to grow than 'Mrs H. Cox', and is nearly as colourful. It is very similar in appearance to 'Skies of Italy' (see page 109), and it is likely that they are often confused with each other.

'Mrs Quilter'
Laing – Britain? 1880
This is a naturally squat, well-branched plant that grows into a nice shape without intervention by the grower. The rounded leaves are golden yellow, with a very prominent chestnut-brown zone. 'Mrs Quilter' makes a magnificent bedding plant, but the small, salmon-pink single flowers are not very freely produced.

'Occold Embers'
S. Stringer – Britain 1977
The large, greenish yellow leaves have a chestnut-brown zone, and are densely produced on a dwarf-growing plant that is self branching and very bushy. The double flowers are a salmon-pink colour.

'Occold Orange Tip'
S. Stringer – Britain date unknown
This is a very unusual miniature cultivar, with white double flowers tipped with orange.

'Orange Fizz'
Blade – country unknown 1965
The large double flowers are a clear orange colour. The plant habit is only moderately bushy and it needs frequent pinching. The leaves are pale green and have no zoning.

'Orange Ricard'
Origin and date unknown
This cultivar is similar to 'Orange Fizz', but the semi-double flowers are a soft, pure orange colour and there is a very faint zone on the leaves. Probably the best orange-flowered, full-sized zonal pelargonium.

'Orion'
S. Stringer – Britain 1964
Another of the Rev. Stringer's miniatures. The leaves are dark green, and the freely produced double flowers are a deep salmon-orange colour.

'Patchwork Quilt'
Raiser and date unknown
The yellowish green leaves have a broad mahogany zone. The plant is very com-pact and bushy, and the single flowers are a deep salmon-pink colour.

'Pink Countess Mariza'
K. Gamble – Britain 1970
This is a sport from 'Countess Mariza' with mauve-pink flowers. All the other characteristics are the same as the parent; 'Pink Countess Mariza' is now the more popular of the two.

'Purple Ball'
W. Elsner – E. Germany date unknown
The double flowers are a bright shade of purple without any tendency to redness. The habit is short jointed, bushy and self branching. Probably the best purple-flowered cultivar available, and it has excellent weather resistance. 'Brook's Purple' has a slightly deeper purple flower, but the plant habit is inferior to that of 'Purple Ball'.

'Red Black Vesuvius'
*Origin uncertain c. 1889 – in Cannell &
Sons list 1890*
The red single flowers are produced very
freely. The leaves are a very dark green
with a black zone, and growth is very
compact. This cultivar is thought by some
to be one of the ancestors of the modern
miniature zonal pelargonium. A sport
from 'Vesuvius'.

'Regina'
Polatschek Bros – Austria 1964
This cultivar won the Prize of Honour at
the 1964 Vienna Exhibition, and has subsequently been used by many hybridists.
'Regina' has given its short jointed, bushy
growth to many new introductions during
the 1970s and 1980s. The large double
flowers are a beautiful pink that deepens to
salmon-pink towards the centre. Despite
the fullness of the blooms it is still a good
bedding plant.

'Royal Norfolk'
S. Stringer – Britain 1976
This cultivar is considered by some to be
the Rev. Stringer's best introduction. The
large double flowers are a glorious shade of
magenta-purple, and the very dark green
leaves are zoned with black. The plant
grows and propagates very well, and with
generous treatment can easily grow to
dwarf stature.

'Scarlet Rambler'
Origin uncertain, possibly USA c. 1878
This is one of the most satisfactory and
attractive members of the Rosebud group.
The tightly packed double flowers are a
brilliant deep red, and the plant habit is
fairly compact and bushy. Also known as
'Red Rosebud' or 'Rosebud Supreme'.

'Schöne Helena'
Fischer – W. Germany c. 1985
This is a large flowered semi-double cultivar, with apricot-pink blooms that have
paler salmon-pink edges. The growth is
very compact, short jointed and bushy. It
is deservedly popular.

'Shimmer'
H. Miller – USA 1958
The double flowers have a shining, silky
appearance, and are a glorious shade of soft
apricot-orange with a silvery reverse. The
leaves are pale green and unzoned, but the
growth is very upright and needs pinching
to encourage bushiness.

'Skelly's Pride'
Cannell & Sons – Britain date unknown
This is an unusual cultivar, which does not
fit into the usual categories. The dark
green leaves have a shiny appearance and
the pale salmon-pink, single flowers have
serrated petal edges. Growth is rather tall
and upright. It is said to be a sport from a
red-flowered cultivar called 'Flame', to
which it sometimes reverts, but it also
reverts to a salmon-flowered plant, presumably 'Salmon Flame'.

'Skies of Italy'
Raiser and date unknown
Descriptions of this cultivar vary greatly.
Some authorities say that it has double
flowers and is synonymous with 'Mrs
Strang'; others believe it is an old cultivar
that has been renamed, or that it is a single
flowered sport of 'Mrs Strang'. The latter
theory seems the most likely, as no doubt
plants labelled 'Skies of Italy' occasionally
revert back to the parent and give rise to
the suggestions of synonymy.

'Snowbaby'
*Case – Britain 1960 (also recorded from
USA)*
The white double flowers are produced on
a miniature plant with olive green leaves.
The flowers sometimes have a greenish
tinge.

'Snowflake'
H. Parrett – Britain date unknown
A miniature with white single flowers.
The leaves are a pleasant mid green colour
and are unzoned.

'Something Special'
E. Popperwell – Britain 1982
The double flowers are a salmon-orange
colour that deepens noticeably in the
centre of each floret; the margins of the
petals are almost white. This is another
'Regina' seedling.

'Scarlet Rambler'
(see page 109)

'Spitfire'

'Spitfire'
Origin and date unknown
This is a member of the cactus flowered group. The bright red petals are rolled up into a quill shape, giving it a novel appearance. The habit of growth is tall and upright, and the leaves are a silvery green with cream-coloured edges.

'Staplegrove Fancy'
Case – Britain c. 1905?
This unusual single flowered cultivar has very variable blooms. The colour is basically white, lightly spotted with a soft reddish pink, especially near the petal edges. The extreme petal edges can sometimes show a solid line of colour. Occasionally the whole flower can be so heavily spotted with red that this becomes the dominant colour. It is very beautiful, but is let down by the tall growing, upright stems. The leaves are pale green and zoneless.

'Sunstar'
S. Stringer – Britain 1967
The large double flowers are an attractive deep orange colour, and are produced on long flower stems. The mid green leaves are noticeably lobed. A miniature.

'Susie Q'
T. Portas – Britain 1976
The medium to large sized leaves are a deep golden yellow with a broad, dark chestnut zone. Like most cultivars of this type the gold colour changes to pale green when the plant has been recently repotted or overfed. The medium to large single flowers are a deep salmon colour. The habit of growth is nicely short jointed and bushy. This cultivar makes an excellent pot plant.

'Treasure Chest'
F. Bode – USA 1965
This is another member of the Irene group, and probably one of the best. The flowers are semi-double and are an unusual shade of orange-scarlet – a distinctly different colour. The growth habit is compact and bushy, and it is an excellent bedding plant.

'Turkish Delight'
I. Gillam – Canada before 1984
The leaves of this very attractive plant have a small central zone of yellow, surrounded by a wide zone of deep brick-red shading to chestnut-brown. The leaf edges are a pale yellowish green. The single flowers are a shining orange-red colour.

'Vina'
A. Shellard – Britain 1983
A very fine dwarf plant. The golden leaves have a diffuse, brownish green zone, and the double flowers are a deep salmon-pink colour lightening towards the petal edges. Very bushy and free flowering. It is difficult to overpraise this excellent cultivar.

SEED-RAISED STRAINS

New seed-raised zonal pelargoniums, or geraniums as most seedsmen refer to them, are constantly being released on to the market. A great deal of money is spent on research and development, so improved strains very quickly replace the existing ones. Only a few of the most up to date cultivars are listed here.

F_I Century series
Colegrave Seeds – Britain 1985
These single flowered cultivars are available in at least nine different colours. They are very uniform in quality; the petal overlay is excellent, and the plants, which branch from the base, produce strong, sturdy stems holding nicely rounded flowerheads well above the foliage.

F_I Diamond series
Walz Seed Co. – W. Germany 1980
These are used by commercial growers to produce packs for massed bedding displays. Packs are trays divided into individual small containers. Plants grown this way are somewhat smaller than normal pot grown plants and are therefore cheaper to produce. The F_1 Diamond series is sold mainly in shades of pink and red.

F_I Video series
Floranova Ltd – Britain before 1983
These are extremely compact plants with dark leaves and very brightly coloured flowers. This strain matures quickly and flowers earlier than many other seed-raised types.

'Balcon Royal'
(see page 112)

Ivy leaf pelargoniums

'Amethyst'
see 'Hillscheider Amethyst'

'Apricot Queen'
Raiser unknown – USA date unknown
This is a strong growing cultivar that needs pinching to encourage bushiness. The leaves are dark green and glossy with a well-marked zone. The double flowers are a deep salmon-pink that noticeably fades first to a clear pink and then to almost white.

'Balcon Royal'
Origin unknown – c. 1960
The flowers of this plant are single and primitive in form, and small plants do not appear to have much to commend them. However, a mature plant can be so prolific in flower that it completely masks the foliage. 'Balcon Royal' has bright red flowers; those of the similar 'King Balcon' and 'Princess Balcon' are salmon and lavender respectively. All of them have originated from 'Ville de Paris'. Closely related plants are the Decora group, which have a similar range of flower colours but stems and leaf petioles that are white rather than green. Cultivars originating from West Germany such as 'Leucht Cascade' ('Fluorescent' or 'Bright Red Cascade') are very similar to the Decora group.

'Barbe Bleu'
Raiser and date unknown
This cultivar has deep blackish purple double flowers; the extreme edges of the petals are a noticeably paler colour. The growth is short and bushy, and the leaves are a bluish shade of green. The translation of the French name is 'Blue Beard'.

'Beauty of Eastbourne'
Listed by Cannell & Sons 1911
The double flowers are a very bright shade of cerise-purple. The growth is moderately compact, but it needs pinching to make a bushy plant. 'Ruben' is similar in appearance but the flower is a slightly paler colour.

'Crocodile'
Raiser unknown – Australia 1964
'Crocodile' and the superficially similar cultivar 'White Mesh' are often confused with each other, and the names are sometimes listed as synonyms. Other names given to these plants are 'Alligator', 'Sussex Lace' and 'Fishnet'. 'Crocodile' has dark green leaves with a yellowish mesh pattern over the whole of the leaf surface. The single flowers are a plum-red colour. 'White Mesh' has a creamy white pattern over the surface of the leaf and deep pink, semi-double flowers.

'Duke of Edinburgh'
Origin and date unknown
The plant currently in cultivation has pink, primitive single flowers with green and white variegated foliage. There is also reference to a cultivar with green and cream leaves and tiny rose-pink double flowers, so there may be more than one cultivar circulating under this name.

'Flakey'
Pat – Canada before 1980
This plant is like a miniature version of 'L'Elegante', but is a sport from 'Gay Baby'. The leaves are a greyish green colour with a white margin and, like those of 'L'Elegante', when the plant is grown dry the leaves become tinged with pink. The small flowers are an off-white colour, but not very freely produced.

'Galilee'
V. Lemoine – France before 1882
One of the oldest cultivars listed in this section, this is still one of the best, especially for outdoor use. The plant is fairly compact, but sufficiently vigorous and spreading to make it ideal for planting in hanging baskets, window boxes, etc. The fully double flowers are a bright pink.

'Green Eyes'
J. Payne – Britain c. 1984
This is a compact, dwarf double flowered cultivar resembling 'Lilac Gem'. The centre of the mauve flower sometimes forms into the shape of a green rosette. Very unusual.

'Harlequin Alpine Glow'

D. Magson – Britain 1982

All the Harlequin series have been produced by a novel grafting method (see
page 63) and have semi-double flowers.
This cultivar is derived from 'Rigi', and
has a deep cerise colour around the edges
of the petals with a central patch of white
heavily streaked with cerise. Growth is
vigorous and spreading.

'Harlequin Mahogany'

D. Magson – Britain 1982

This Harlequin is derived from 'Yale', and
is white with a bold cherry-red border
around each petal. The colour is distinct
from the similarly marked 'Rouletta', and
is probably the most eyecatching and
satisfactory member of this group. (See
also 'Harlequin Alpine Glow'.)

'Harlequin Picotee'

D. Magson – Britain 1982

The flower is nearly white but has a
picotee edge of light candy pink; the
spreading stems are rather thin. This Harlequin has 'Galilee' as a parent. (See also
'Harlequin Alpine Glow'.)

'Harlequin Rosie O'Day'

D. Magson – Britain 1982

The petals are heavily edged in deep cerise-
pink and the centre of the petals are white,
very heavily striped and flecked with
cerise-pink. This cultivar was derived
from 'Super Rose'. (See also 'Harlequin
Alpine Glow'.)

'Hillscheider Amethyst'

W. Elsner – E. Germany date unknown

The very fully double flowers are a deep
shade of lavender-purple. The plant
growth is very compact and bushy, and
the leaves are well zoned. It is not usually
listed under the full name but under
'Amethyst', so care must be taken not to
confuse it with the regal pelargonium
called 'Amethyst', or the similarly coloured ivy leaf pelargonium 'Dunkle
Amethyst' ('Dresdner Dunkle
Amethyst').

'La France'

Listed by Cannell & Sons 1900

'La France' is a vigorous plant that will
produce long, trailing stems; it has large,
lavender-coloured, semi-double flowers.

'L'Elegante'

Listed by Cannell & Sons 1868

The habit of this plant is nearly dwarf, and
if it is grown on the dry side the internodal
distance will be short and the greyish
green, cream-edged leaves take on a purplish red hue. The white single flowers are
primitive in form but are produced in
great profusion. This is deservedly a very
popular cultivar, and looks well even if
badly neglected.

'Lilac Gem'

Origin and date unknown

The plant has a very compact, dwarf habit
and the dark green, shiny leaves smell
strongly of ivy (*Hedera* spp.). The lilac-
coloured double flowers are very freely
produced. Sometimes listed as 'Mauve
Beauty'.

'Pink Mini Cascade'

Fischer – W. Germany date unknown

The small, pink, primitive flowers are
profusely produced on a dwarf, free branching plant. Rather like a dwarf version of
'King Balcon', though the flowers of the
latter plant are more salmon in colour.
Also known as 'Rosa Mini Cascade'.

'Pink Snowdrift'

D. Clark – Britain 1987

This is a candy pink sport from 'Snowdrift'. Like that of its parent, the growth is
rather open and spreading; this makes it a
good subject for a hanging basket. The
double flowers occasionally produce green
centres.

'Red Mini Cascade'

Fischer – W. Germany date unknown

The primitive single flowers are a bright
red colour, and the dwarf plant is compact
and self branching. Best grown on the dry
side. A small plant looks unpromising but
on maturing it develops into a spectacular
specimen. Very good for outside use in
planters, window boxes, etc. Rather like a
dwarf version of 'Balcon Royal'. Sometimes seen as 'Rote Mini Cascade'.

'L'Elegante' (see page 113)

'Rio Grande'

'Rigi'
Origin and date unknown
The very large semi-double flowers are a luminous lilac colour. The growth is vigorous, and the leaves are dark green with a small black zone.

'Rio Grande'
I. Parsons – Britain 1982
The double flowers are almost black – together with 'Barbe Bleu', probably the nearest to black in this group of plants. Growth is vigorous, rather sprawling and long jointed.

'Rouletta'
Raiser unknown – Mexico c. 1970
This cultivar occurred as a chance sport from 'Mexican Beauty', and spread rapidly around the world. The semi-double flowers are white, with a cerise-red edge to the petals; a very striking combination. It has also been listed as 'Mexicanerin' and 'Mexicana'. The growth is long and inclined to be straggly, so the growing tips should be pinched frequently to help create a more bushy plant.

'Snowdrift'
Raiser unknown – USA 1962
This cultivar has a nearly pure white double flower, but the flower buds and the centre of the open flower have a greenish tinge. Slender, rather sprawling growth.

'Snow Queen' ('Schneekönigin')
Fischer – W. Germany 1976
The double white flowers have small red markings in the centre. The growth habit is compact and very bushy. (There is also a cactus flowered zonal pelargonium called 'Snow Queen' that was introduced in 1907.)

'Sugar Baby'
Crane – USA 1964
This is a splendid dwarf, with very bushy stems that are densely covered with mid green leaves, and double candy pink flowers produced in great profusion. The habit of the plant is bushy rather than trailing.

'Sybil Holmes'
Raiser unknown – USA date unknown
Very compact and bushy growth; this cultivar is almost dwarf. The pink flowers are very fully double, rather like small rosebuds. 'Ailsa Garland' is synonymous; slight variations in the flower colours can be attributed to differences in cultivation.

'Tavira'
Raiser and date unknown
The semi-double flowers are a bright red colour. The growth habit is well branching and bushy, but will still produce long, trailing stems. At the time of writing this is generally regarded as the best red-

flowered ivy leaf pelargonium. It almost certainly originated in Belgium, and was renamed 'Tavira' when introduced into Britain in 1969/70 by Wyck Hill Geraniums. It has subsequently been exported around the world – including its country of origin – under its new name.

'White Mesh'
Raiser and date unknown
The flowers are semi-double and a deep pink colour, but the main attractions are the cream-veined green leaves. A similar cultivar is 'Crocodile', but is has deep red single flowers.

'Yale'
Raiser and date unknown
This cultivar has deep, velvety red semi-double flowers – a glorious colour, let down by very long, straggling stems. It is an attractive plant if grown in a large hanging basket situated where the long stems have plenty of room to develop. It is almost certainly of American origin, as it was named after Yale University. It has also been listed as 'Old Lady'.

HYBRID IVY LEAF PELARGONIUMS

'Elsi'
Raiser unknown – possibly Australia
c. 1965
An upright growing plant that sprawls with age. Best kept well pinched when young to encourage bushy growth. The double flowers are crimson, and the leaves are a silvery green colour with cream edges.

'Harlequin Pretty Girl'
D. Magson – Britain 1982
This is a semi-upright growing plant with rather pale green leaves. The petals have white centres and are boldly bordered with bright orange. This very attractive plant is derived from 'Schöne von Grenchen'. (See also 'Harlequin Alpine Glow', page 113.)

'Magaluf'
N. Watkins – Britain 1982
The foliage is silvery green with a cream

edge, and the pink single flowers have crimson spots on the upper petals. This plant was found as a sport growing on a green-leaved plant on a rubbish tip in Spain.

'Millfield Gem'
V. Lemoine – France 1894
An old cultivar, but still the standard by which others in this group are judged. The large semi-double or double flowers are a very pale pink colour, spotted and streaked with red on the upper petals.

'Sugar Baby'

'Tavira'

Tables of Recommendations

PELARGONIUMS FOR EXHIBITION

REGAL PELARGONIUMS

'Amethyst'
'Aztec'
'Beryl Reid'
'Grand Slam'
'Hazel Cherry'
'Hazel Gypsy'
'Hazel Herald'
'Hazel Perfection'
'Lavender Grand Slam'
'Lavender Harewood Slam'

'Monkwood Bonanza'
'Monkwood Delight'
'Pink Bonanza'
'Purple Rogue'
'Rosmaroy'
'Spot On Bonanza'
'Sunrise' (as a 2-year-old plant)
'Vicky Town'
'White Bonanza'

ZONAL PELARGONIUMS

'Blues'
'Bold Appleblossom'
'Brenda Kitson'
'Burgenlandmadel'
'Contrast'
'Countess Mariza'
'Freak of Nature'
'Highfield's Choice'
'Highfield's Festival'

'Highfield's Pride'
'Mars'
'Miss Burdett-Coutts'
'Mrs H. Cox'
'Pink Countess Mariza'
'Regina'
'Schöne Helena'
'Something Special'
'Treasure Chest'

DWARF ZONAL PELARGONIUMS

'Deacon Bonanza'
'Deacon Lilac Mist'
'Emma Hossler'

'Frank Headley'
'Morval'
'Vina'

MINIATURE ZONAL PELARGONIUMS

'Fleurette'   'Miss Wackles'
'Goblin'   'Orion'
'Jane Eyre'   'Royal Norfolk'
'Marmalade'

IVY LEAF PELARGONIUMS

'Barbe Bleu'   'Lilac Gem'
'Flakey'   'Red Mini Cascade'
'Galilee'   'Snow Queen'
'Hillscheider Amethyst'   'Sugar Baby'
'L'Elegante'   'Sybil Holmes'

ZONAL PELARGONIUMS FOR GROWING AS UNGRAFTED STANDARDS

'Caroline Schmidt'   'Distinction'
'Deacon Bonanza'   'Frank Headley'
'Deacon Peacock'   'Irene'

Glossary

anther The pollen-bearing part at the tip of a stamen.

axil The point where a leaf joins the stem, from which new growth or flowers emerge.

break To send out new growth. This can occur by pinching out the growing tip of a stem, or as the result of vigorous pruning of an old stem or of new growth produced at the end of the dormant season.

cultivar A cultivated plant that has reached its present form through the intervention of man, as distinct from a variety that occurs naturally in the wild. Abbreviated to cv.

damping off A term used to describe the death of a cutting or seedling by an unknown fungal disease, usually caused by unclean materials or tools and made worse by a close, damp atmosphere.

dormancy A temporary state of rest that can be induced by withholding water for a period and allowing the temperature to fall so that, in the case of a deciduous plant, the leaves fall.

family A group of genera with important characteristics in common, e.g. Geraniaceae, geranium family.

filament The stalk of an anther; together they form the stamen.

floret Small individual flowers of a dense inflorescence.

genus A group of species with important characteristics in common, e.g. *Pelargonium*.

Opposite: Traditional red zonal pelargoniums bringing cheer to a street in France

Left: 'Frank Headley' (see page 104)

hybrid A cross between different species, subspecies or varieties.

inflorescence The flowering part of the plant.

internode The length of stem between nodes.

meristem A zone of actively dividing cells that occurs at the root and shoot tips.

node The point on a stem where the leaves arise.

ovary The female portion of a flower, which contains embryonic seeds (ovules) that are fertilized by the pollen.

pedicel The stalk of an individual flower or fruit in an inflorescence.

peduncle The stalk of a solitary flower or cluster of flowers.

pinch out To remove the growing tip of a stem using thumbnail and forefinger. The tip can also be cut out using a sharp knife or other instrument. It has essentially the same meaning as stopping.

pip One single flower or floret.

pistil The ovary, style and stigma.

pot back To shake old soil from a plant and to replant with fresh compost into a smaller pot. This process is often carried out at the end or start of a growing season.

pot on To remove the plant into a larger container with as little disturbance to the roots as possible.

re-pot To shake off old soil from the roots and replant with fresh compost into the same sized or a larger pot. The terms re-pot and pot on have very different meanings and should not be confused.

soft growth Young growth that has not yet hardened or matured.

species A group of plants that have essentially the same characteristics and are (or were) found in the wild and that come true from seed. Abbreviated to sp. (singular) and spp. (plural).

sport A mutation that occurs in a bud, which then develops to give a plant with a differently coloured flower or perhaps variegated leaves. This mutation can arise spontaneously or be induced artificially.

stamen The male organ of a flower.

stigma The tip of the pistil that receives the pollen.

stipule An often leafy appendage at the base of some petioles.

stop To stop a stem is synonymous with pinching out.

style The stalk of the stigma, which connects it to the ovary.

succulent A plant that is adapted to withstand dryness and stores water by means of swollen or fleshy stems, leaves or tuberous roots.

taxon A taxonomic group of any ranks, e.g. genus, species, cultivar, etc.

umbel An inflorescence in which the individual flower stalks or pedicels, come from the tip of the peduncle, e.g. the inflorescence of a pelargonium.

variety A distinct form of a species, but of insufficient importance to justify it as a separate species or subspecies.

woody growth The older woody or brown parts of the lower stem.

Bibliography

The following publications are suitable for the amateur pelargonium grower.

Bagust, Harold *Miniature Geraniums* (John Gifford, 1969)
Clark, D. W. H. *The Oakleigh Guide to Geraniums (Pelargoniums)* (Oakleigh Publications, 1986)
Clifford, D. *Pelargoniums including the popular 'Geranium'* (Blandford Press, 1970)
Key, Hazel *Pelargoniums, Wisley Handbook No. 18* (Cassell Ltd/RHS 1985)
Llewellyn, J., Hudson, B., & Morrison, G. C. *Growing Geraniums and Pelargoniums* (Kangaroo Press, 1984)
Shellard, Alan *Geraniums for Home and Garden* (David & Charles, 1981)
Shellard, Alan *Growing and Showing Geraniums* (David & Charles, 1984)
Witham-Fogg, H. G. *Geraniums and Pelargoniums* (John Gifford, 1975)
Wood, H. J. *Pelargoniums. A Complete Guide to Their Cultivation* (Faber & Faber, 1966)

The following works are more suited to botanists or to the more dedicated grower.

Walt, van der, J. A. A. *Pelargoniums of Southern Africa 1* (Purnell & Sons S.A. (Pty) Ltd, 1977)
Walt, van der, J. A. A., Vorster, P. J. *Pelargoniums of Southern Africa 2.* (Juta & Co. Ltd, 1981)
Webb, W. J. *The Pelargonium Family. The Species of Pelargonium, Monsonia and Sarcocaulon* (Croom Helm, 1984)

Curtis's *Botanical Magazine* (now *The Kew Magazine*). This publication still maintains its long tradition of fine colour printing and articles on plants, plant collecting and conservation. Since it was established in 1787 nearly 10,500 colour plates have appeared by many of the best British botanical artists.

Acknowledgements

The author gratefully acknowledges the assistance of the following people and societies who generously supplied information used in the preparation of this book: Mrs M. Furze and the other members of the Nomenclature Committee of the British Pelargonium and Geranium Society; Mr A. Pearce of Fareham and Mr J. Thorp of Wokingham; Mr M. D. Grisley of Hornchurch, who kindly provided much information on 'oil of geranium'; Mr H. Weller of the British and European Geranium Society, who gave unselfishly from his extensive knowledge and greatly assisted in tracking down the origins of some of the more obscure cultivars; Dr P. J. Vorster of the University of Stellenbosch, South Africa, for his assistance over some of the species; and Colegrave Seeds of Banbury, for providing background information and details of seed-raised strains.

Line artwork by Ron Hayward

Photographs
Pat Brindley, pages 38, 83, 87; Crown copyright © reproduced with the permission of the Controller, Her Majesty's Stationary Office, and the Director, Royal Botanic Gardens, Kew, pages 10, 14; The Hamlyn Publishing Group Ltd/William Davidson, page 78; Andrew Lawson, page 66; Photos Horticultural, pages 6, 19, 34; Octopus, page 54; The Harry Smith Horticultural Photographic Collection, pages 26, 42, 86, 90–1. All other photographs by David Clark.

Taxonomy checked by Susyn Andrews, who works as a botanist at The Royal Botanic Gardens, Kew, and is also a member of the Kew Magazine Editorial Committee.

Index